Captain George W. Kimball. Taken about 1870.

ANTIOCH TO THE TWENTIES

Second Edition

REVISED AND EXPANDED

ELISE S. BENYO

 Published by Byron Hot Springs, San Francisco, California
https://byronhotsprings.com

Copyright © 2024 Byron Hot Springs. All rights reserved.
License to reprint *Antioch to the Twenties* (1972) by Elise S. Benyo.
Copyright © 1987 by Michael S. Benyo granted by the Estate of Michael S. Benyo.

Library of Congress Control Number: 2024938402

Book design and composition by Maureen Forys, Happenstance Type-O-Rama
Front cover image by Chantelle Leighton
Index by Ken DellaPenta

Second Edition: Revised and Expanded

Printed in the United States of America in compliance with the Lacey Act by Ingram® Lightning Source®

For general information, reviews and corrections please contact:
historian@byronhotsprings.com

Disclaimer: All content errors and omissions are the responsibility of the author. Original grammar, syntax, punctuation and capitalization as edited to conform to modern standards are the responsibility of the publisher.

1971 DEDICATION

TO THE PAST
Captain George W. Kimball
Adelia B. Kimball Schott
Franklin T. Schott

THE PRESENT
Michael S.
Catherine
Helen

THE FUTURE
Julie
Marcia
Jack Michael

View of the Antioch riverfront during the age of sail (1909).

FOREWORD

Dear Reader:

Elise Benyo knew it was important work when she began *Antioch to the Twenties*. The town was more than 120-years-old at its writing, her adopted hometown and birthplace of most of her students. All townspeople knew that Antioch was an important commercial, manufacturing and shipping location. Little did they realize its important commerce role in both the Mexican, Gold Rush, and early California statehood periods.

All pioneers instinctively knew that land located at the junction of two mighty rivers is the key to commercial success. Antioch is uniquely established at the junction of California's two major rivers, the Sacramento and the San Joaquin. Here, men and material passed upriver to the Mother Lode. Ore and agricultural products moved downriver to San Francisco to finance and feed the world. Dreams traveled both directions ensuring Antioch's importance from its founding in 1848.

The first pioneer to settle the interior of California and establish his rancho far from the existing coastal communities was John Marsh in 1837. At that time, Santa Clara, Yerba Buena and Monterey all held missions and presidios bristling with military might. No security existed on the "opposite shore" or the "Contra Costa" where mountain men reigned in the fur trade and Marsh held 40,000 acres east of Mount Diablo. Eleven years after establishing his fiefdom, Marsh offered brothers William and Joseph Smith a parcel of land to settle at the junction of the Sacramento and San Joaquin rivers for $500.00. The town was born. Coincidentally, this was the same dollar amount Marsh paid José Noriega for Rancho los Megeños de los Polpones in 1837.

This new community, initially named "Smith's Landing," was soon renamed "Antioch" by its settlers in honor of the Biblical Palestine city. As such, Antioch is not only the oldest city in Contra Costa County, it competes with rival Sacramento City as the oldest city in California in the American era. San Diego, Monterey, San Juan Capistrano and San Francisco all date to the Spanish and Mexican colonial periods (1776 to 1848). Antioch and Sacramento City rank within the first 10 cities established in California by European colonists and both predate statehood (1850).

If not for Elise Benyo's effort, research and writing our history would not be as accessible today for students, parents, residents, or planning departments. History counts! *Antioch to the Twenties* should be on everyone's reading list. Thank you, Elise!

Sincerely,

CAROL A. JENSEN
Editor

Antioch School building (1910), teachers and students.

CONTENTS

1971 Dedication . . . . *v*
Foreword . . . . *vii*
Preface to the First Edition . . . . *x*
Key of Locations on Map of Area about 1880 . . . . *xi*
Map of the Area 1830 . . . . *xii*
Map of Antioch 1900 . . . . *xiv*
Key for the Antioch Map . . . . *xvi*
Significant Dates in Antioch History . . . . *xviii*
1971 Acknowledgements . . . . *xix*
1971 Board of Education . . . . *xx*

PART I

Early Beginning and City Development 1
Map of the Coal Mine Railroad 1860–1903 28

PART II

Industry 31

PART III

Educational, Spiritual and Social Life 57
Homes—Then and Now 78

PART IV

Farming, Produce and Climate 85

Bibliography *101*
Selected Reading *103*
Index *105*
About the Author of Antioch to the Twenties *115*
About the Antioch Historical Society *116*

PREFACE
to the First Edition

Antioch has always held a great fascination for me since the days when I was a child in Salt Lake City when my father told me of his boyhood experiences in Antioch. I became extremely interested in the early beginnings of Antioch when we broke up my father's home on Third Street in 1939. I became much aware of the desirability to collect these experiences and bits of information into a lasting form. In preparing the celebration material for Antioch's Centennial, I found there was no real source material available. This book is a collection of thoughts, ideas, anecdotes, notations, experiences and reprints of documents of the past. I have only acted as the collector. I am attempting to put things into a form that will be of interest to the reader. Above all, I hope to let the students, elementary or secondary, feel that the people living through the past had failure, success, sadness and happiness, much as we do today.

If I have eliminated individuals or families that should have been included, it has been inadvertent. I am sorry for any such omission and would appreciate hearing about them. I have had to depend on people to share with me their memories and collections of the Antioch past.

I wish to thank everyone who has helped me in any way. Please realize that without all of you, this collection would not have been possible. This is a part of many people and their relations who called Antioch home during the first four score years of Antioch's development.

My special thanks to Ralph and Anna Beede, Jean Turner, Mr. Albert Scott, Mr. Albert Flaherty, Mr. Wm. Tornheim, and those members of the Antioch School District whose encouragement and hours of work with me kept me going, to my husband Michael, who kept reminding me to do my best and was so patiently understanding while I was "digging".

E.S.B.
Antioch, 1971

KEY OF LOCATIONS
on Map of Area about 1880

TOWNS OR SETTLEMENTS
1. San Francisco
2. San Rafael
3. Oakland
4. Alameda
5. Stege (Richmond)
6. Vallejo
7. Benicia
8. Martinez
9. Concord
10. Walnut Creek
11. Lafayette
12. Danville
11. Livermore
14. Cowell
15. Dublin
16. Alamo
17. Port Costa
18. Pittsburg
20. Antioch
21. Byron
22. Brentwood
22. Oakley
24. Knightsen
25. Carquinez (Crockett)
26. Hayward
27. Clayton
28. Pacheco
29. San Pablo
30. San Ramon
31. Pinole
32. Nortonville
34. Judsonville

LANDMARKS/ GEOGRAPHIC POINT
A. Golden Gate
B. San Francisco Bay
C. San Pablo Bay
D. Suisun Bay
E. Sacramento River
F. San Joaquin River
G. Sherman Island
H. Kimball Island
I. Mare Island
J. Yuebra [Sic Yerba] Buena
K. The Delta Islands
   I. Bradford
   II. Webb Tract
   III. Jersey
   IV. Bethel
   V. Holland
   VI. Palm and Orwood Tracts
   VII. Frank's Track (undated)
L. Los Medaños Grant
M. The Point (Smith's)
N. Marsh Landing
O. Babbe Landing
P. Iron House Landing
R. Point of' Timber
S. Dr. Marsh House
T. Carquinez Straits
U. Browns Island
W. Chipps Island
X. Pittsburg or Black Diamond Landing
Y. New York Landing
Z. Winter Island

COAL MINES/ RAILROADS
San Pablo & Tulare Railroad 1878
Southern Pacific

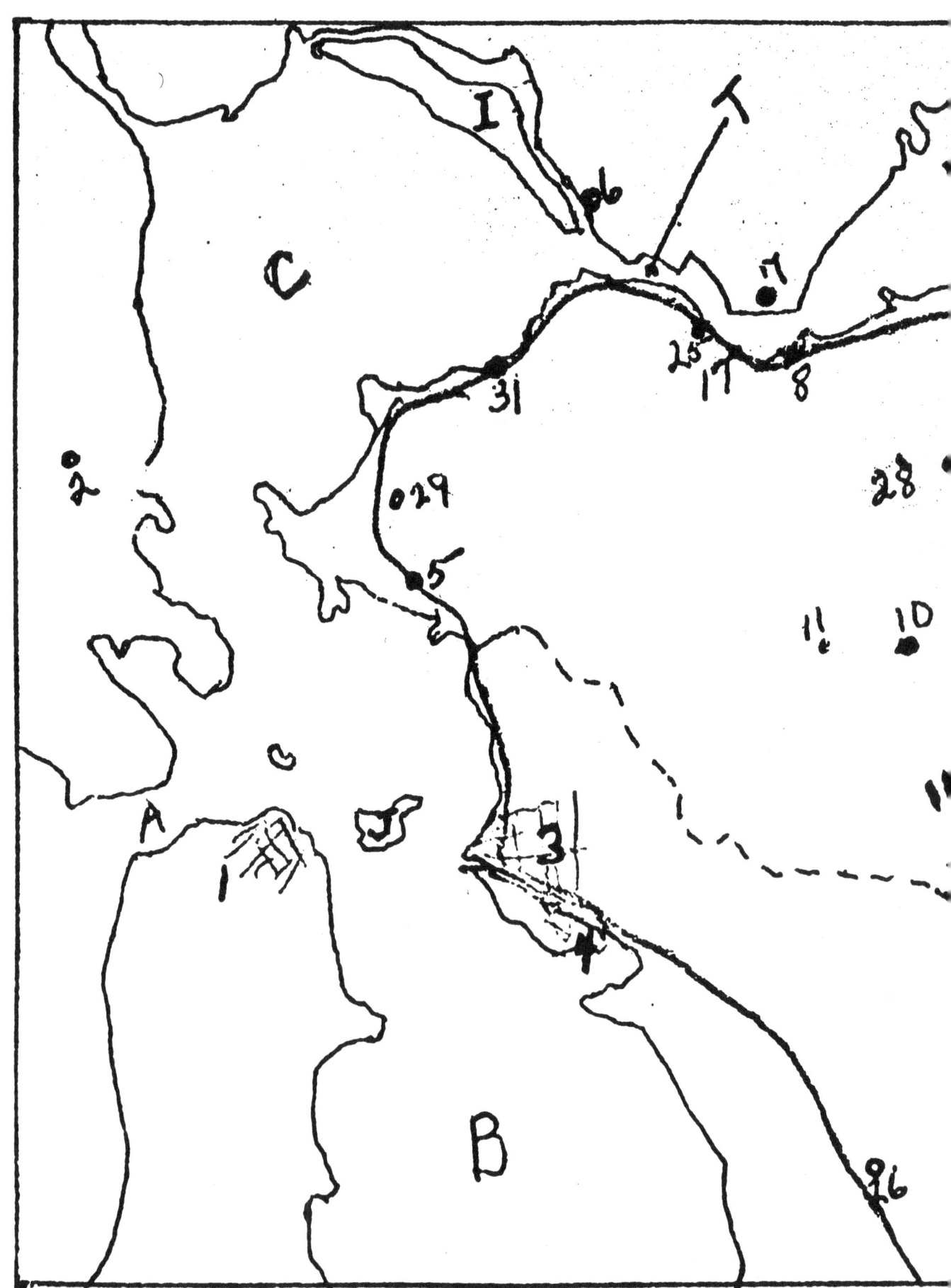

Map of the Area about 1880

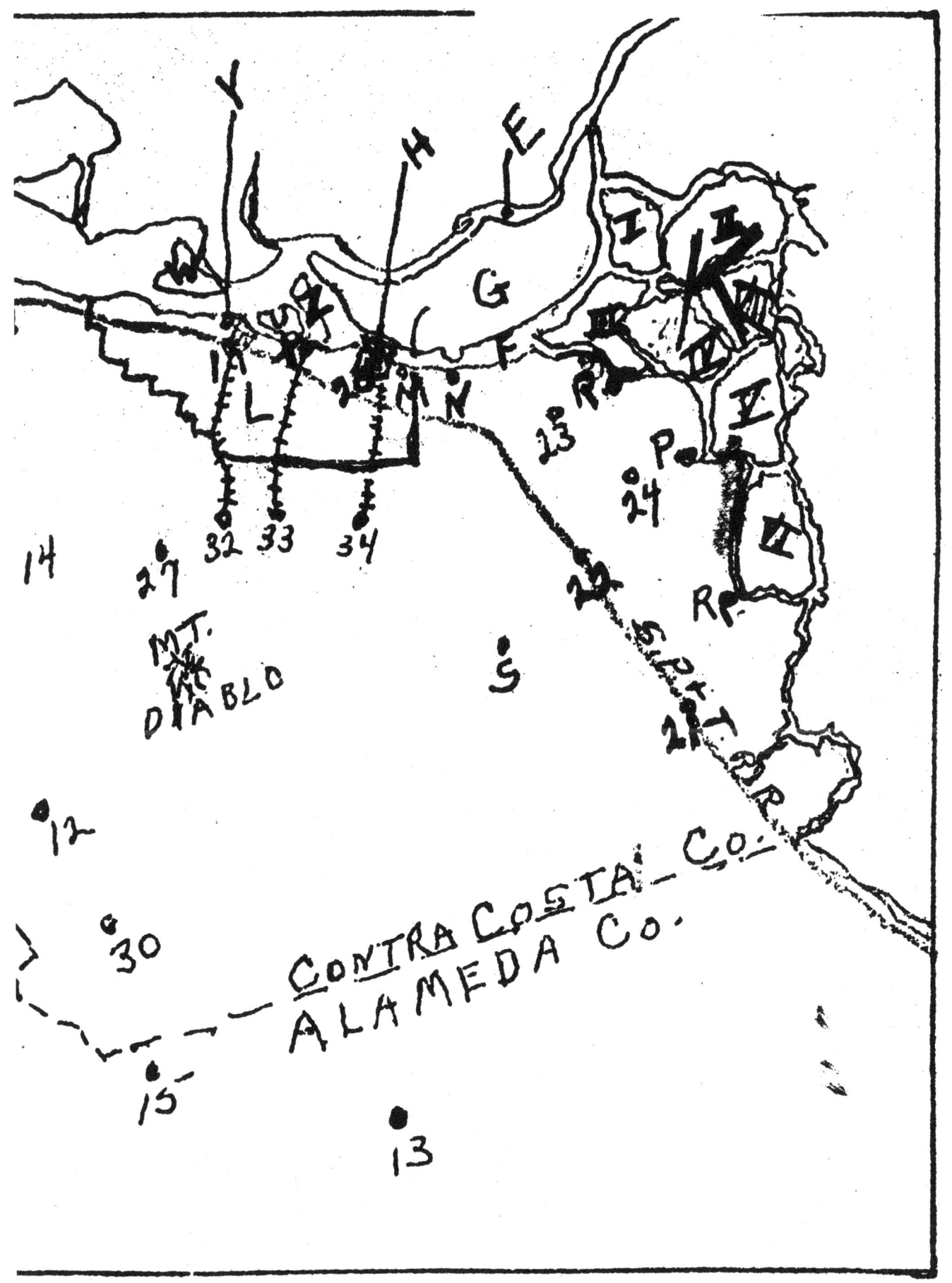

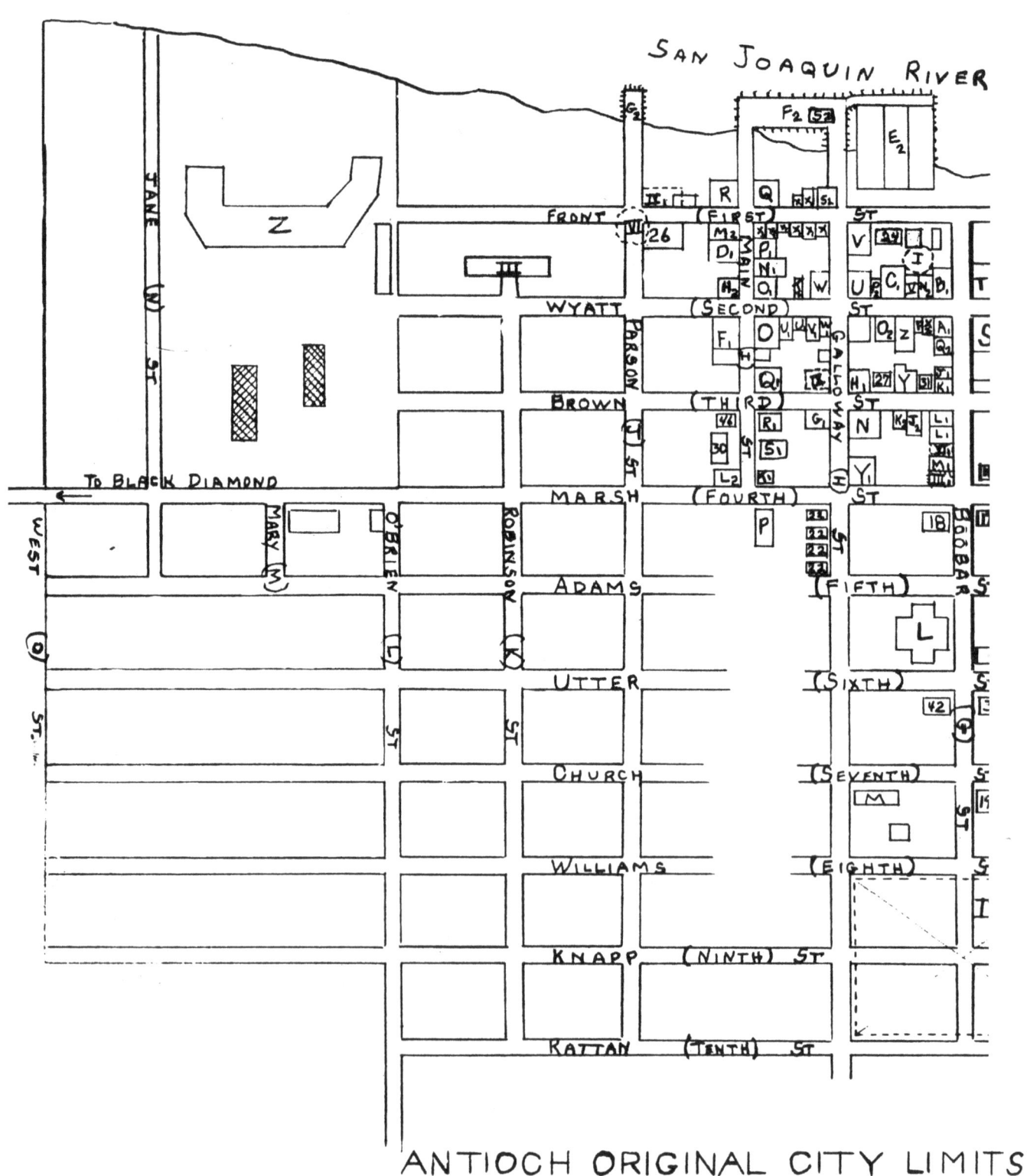

Map of Antioch Original City Limits and Buildings to 1900

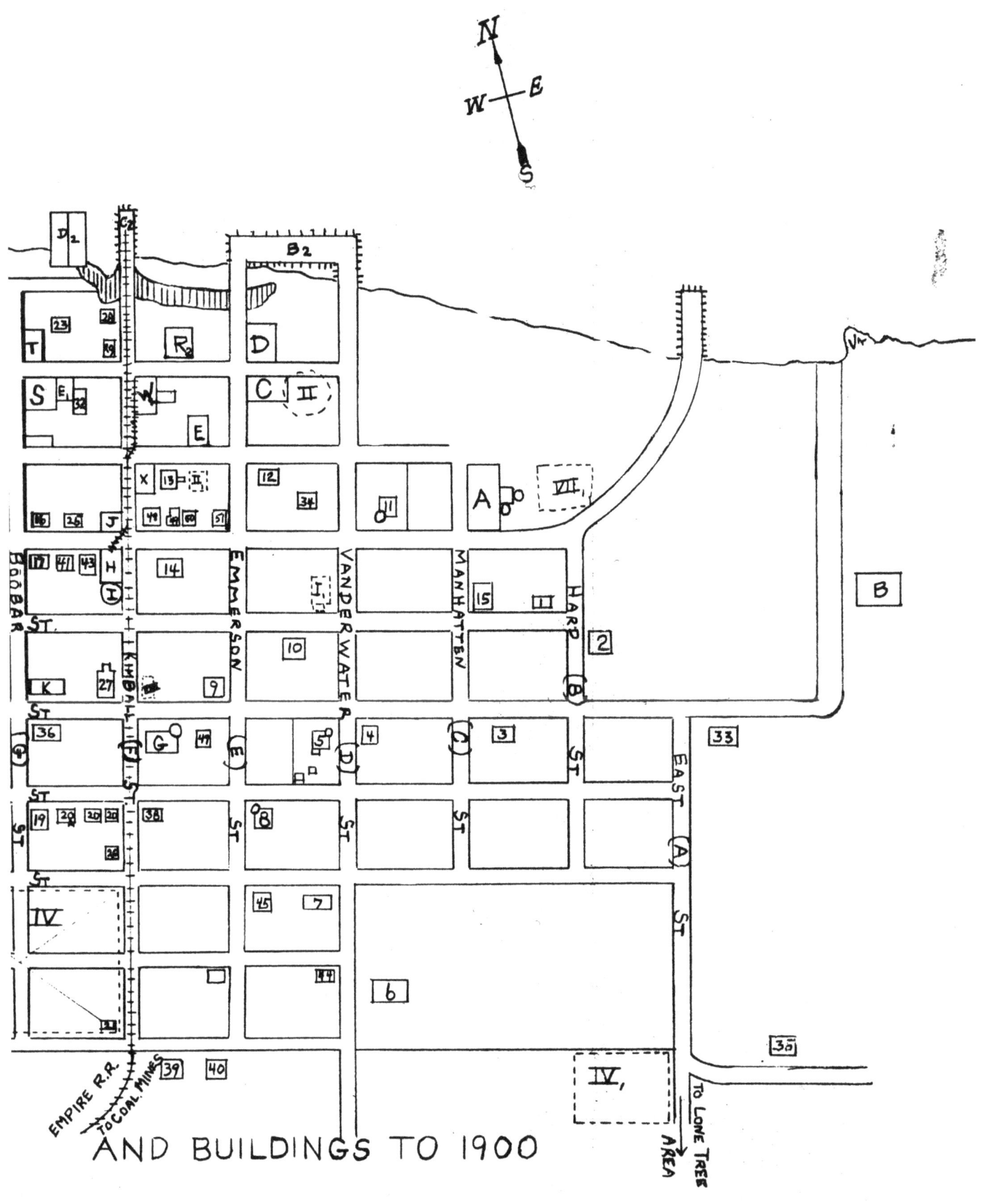

KEY OF LOCATIONS
on Antioch Map

HOMES IN ANTIOCH INDICATING BUILDER OR FIRST OWNER
1. Luddinghouse-Wall
2. Ferd Stamm
3. John Thomas Cox
4. Nason, Brown, R. Beede
5. Dr. George
6. T. N. Wills
7. Waldie
8. C. H. Belshaw
9. Remfree
10. G. Meyers
11. Harkinson
12. Abbott
13. Kimball
14. Harkinson
15. Hawxhurst
16. Keeney
17. J. T. Belshaw
18. C. Marsh, Hartley
19. Dunnigan
20. Built by J. R. Baker
20. A. J. Rio Baker
21. A. B. Schott, L. Meyers
22. Built by G. and M. Field
23. Carman, Dr. Moore
24. Galloway, Rouse
25. McGrath
26. Hard, Noakes
27. McKellips
28. W. Forman
29. Pitts
30. Dr. DeWitt
31. Donlon
32. Montgomery
33. W. W. Smith
34. Hutchison
35. H. F. Beede built by Sloan
36. Worrell
37. Peterson
38. Hale
39. Dr. Wemple
40. Dr. Wemple's Barn, then Dr. Rattan
41. Cooney
42. Heath
43. Bullock
44. Wilkening, Thyarks
45. Caple
46. McGuire
47. Builder Unknown
48. Cleaves
49. Built by Hill
50. Built by Hill and F. Cooney
51. W. Turner

I. Picnic Area of 1851
II. Brick Kiln
III. Albion Pottery
IV. Cemetery to 1882
V. First Ledger Office
VI. First Brick Kiln
I. Future Christian Science Church
II. Future home of Mrs. A. B. Schott
III. Future Telephone Office
IV. Future City Park
V. Future Santa Fe Depot
VI. Future Otto Klengel Build Inc.
VII. Future Planing Mill
VIII. Future Library
IX. Future City Hall

BUSINESS LOCATIONS OF ANTIOCH
A. Distillery
B. Pottery works (east of Antioch)
C. Lumber Shed
D. Grange Hall later Antioch Lumber Office
E. Luddinghouse Blacksmith and Carriage Makers
F. Barber Shop (Azevedo)
G. Congregational Church
H. Empire Railroad Roundhouse and Blacksmith
I. Water Tower
J. Klengel Store (brother of Otto) and (H. B. Reed Funeral Home)
K. Methodist Church
L. School, Brick later Frame
M. Catholic Church
N. Union Hall and City Bakery, later I.O.O.F and Masons met there
O. Griffith Hotel or American Exchange and Wash House (destroyed in fire of 1871)
P. Christian Advent Church
Q. Carmen and Isreal Store

R. Homberg Store and Hall
S. Belshaw Store later Belshaw Theatre
T. Brown & Baker Hardware
U. First Lumber Office later Bank of America
V. Lumber Warehouse later Casino Theater
W. Kimball Dry Goods later Deyer's Store
X. Scout's Hall
Y. City Hall and Jail
Z. Drug Store and O'Brien Hall

A1. Joslin Harness Shop later First National Bank
B1. Palace Hotel later El Campanil
C1. Dickerson later Arlington Hotel
D1. Tyler Hotel
E1. Ledger Office after 1882
F1. Antioch Hotel later Arata Building Commercial Hotel
G1. Madame LeGuevelis Milliner Dress Shop
H1. Peterson's Blacksmith Shop
J1. Ross Ice Cream Store
K1. Joe Ross Grocery (Donlon Home was moved.)
L1. Donlon Drayage Building (two cow sheds to the south)
M1. Hunter's Stable (burned)
N1. Chinese Church
O1. National Hall
P1. Kelley Funeral Home
Q1. Chase and Robbins Livery Stable (destroyed in fire of 1871)
R1. McCoy's Two-story Shop and Home (destroyed in fire of 1871)
S1. D. Cleaves home (destroyed in fire of 1871)
T1. Vacant Home (Knapp lived there before home destroyed by fire in 1871)
U1. McCartney's Home and Variety Story (destroyed in fire of 1871)
V1. Tapperner's Shoe Store (destroyed in fire of 1871)
W1. Hop Lee's Wash House (torn down to stop the fire of 1871)
X1. Chinese homes
Y1. Livery Stable

A2. Distillery Wharf
B2. Lumber Wharf
C2. Coal Wharf
D2. Hay Warehouse
E2. Grain Warehouse
F2. Antioch Wharf
G2. Smith Mail Wharf later Municipal Wharf
H2. Il Figaro Barber
J2. Wol Kahn & Co. General Mercantile
K2. R. Keddy - Surveyor
L2. S. Jessup
M2. Jacobs General Dry Goods
N2. Stamm Bros. Shoes and Boots
O2. Klengel Harness Shop
P2. Wall Store (Shoes)
Q2. Hartley Building, Dr. DeWitt (Express Office)
R2. Joe Cervans Machine Shop
S2. Antioch Wharf, Fred Dalinker-Wharfinger, Gillpatrick's Express
T2. Arata Grocery
U2. Blacksmith Shop
V2. The Point
W2. Empire Yards
X2. Home Bakery

SIGNIFICANT DATES IN ANTIOCH HISTORY

1849 Town site acquired from Dr. John Marsh, first medical doctor in California.

1851 July 4, town named "Antioch" at a picnic held by the river, "Because Christ's disciples were first called Christians at Antioch."

1853 Shipping wharf built. The principal means of transportation of this period was by water.

1853 to 1880 With 3 miles of water frontage 40-feet deep, Antioch became the furthest inland shipping center for ocean going vessels with cargo bound for central Ca1ifornia.

1854 A lumber company established at 2nd and E streets. Now Antioch Lumber Company, the oldest, continuously operating business in Contra Costa County.

1870 Publication begins of a weekly newspaper, the *Antioch Ledger*, published continuously since the town of Antioch incorporated.

1871 A fire, fanned by a north wind, burned three city blocks of downtown Antioch to the ground in 40 minutes.

1878 The Southern Pacific Railroad (now Amtrack) built through Antioch.

1889 The first paper mill built. Paper production was for many years the leading industry of Antioch. (Fibreboard and Crown Zellerbach)

1892 The first telephone exchange opened serving six subscribers. By 1898, the number of subscribers grew to 33.

1900 A second railroad, the Santa Fe (now Amtrack), reached Antioch.

1919 Former Antioch City Hall built this date and demolished in 1981.

1926 The Antioch Bridge opened. It was the very first of eight highway bridges built over San Francisco Bay Area waterways.

1981 The new John Nejedly Bridge replaced the old Antioch Bridge.

1981 The new 3-story City Hall with Council Chambers and Regional Communication Center built (Grand Opening December 5, 1981).

2022 City of Antioch Sesquicentennial (1872–1922) celebration.

Information provided by the Antioch Historical Society.

1971 ACKNOWLEDGEMENTS

The Antioch Unified School District will forever be indebted to Mrs. Elise Benyo for her outstanding contribution of the history of this community. The book will be used as a teaching tool in our social studies program for our elementary schools and as a reference source in our secondary schools. To Mrs. Benyo, we say thanks. To her fellow co-workers and future teachers of Antioch, we present this book to you.

1971 BOARD OF EDUCATION
Mrs. Joy Motts, Chairman
Robert Hutchison, Vice Chairman
Mrs. Mary Rocha
Earl Taylor
John Tilden
Robert N. Kennedy, Superintendent of Schools
Frank C. Burk, Assistant Superintendent for Instruction

[Editor's note: The publisher wishes to thank the following individuals and organizations for their kind assistance in making this long out-of-print, local history book available to the next generation. Helen E. Hagstrom, daughter of Elise S. Benyo; Sheri Gayle, President, Antioch Historical Society; Dwayne Eubanks, President Emeritus, Antioch Historical Society; Lucy Meinhardt, Board Member, Antioch Historical Society; Barry Delavan, Member, Antioch Historical Society; Antioch Historical Society general membership; Maureen Forys, Happenstance Type-O-Rama; Chantelle Leighton, Chantelle Designs; Karel Ancona, Moonbean Publishing; Diana Thomas, proofreader; Ken DellaPenta, Index Services; Tim Runk, Proprietor, Publisher's Prepress; and the irreplaceable Robert D. Haines, deceased, Argonaut Book Shop.]

Antioch Train Depot, Sante Fe Railway (1907).

PART I

Early Beginnings and City Development

The brothers Reverends William Wiggin Smith (b. 1811 d. 1899) and Rev. Joseph Horton Smith (b. 1811 d. 1850) left Boston harbor aboard the brig, *Forest*, for the Golden State, January 11, 1849, accompanied by their wives, J. C. McMaster and 50 others. The Smiths' early years had been spent in study in New Hampshire. Rev. William Smith had been placed as a regular bound apprentice to a carpenter and housebuilder. Rev. Joseph Smith was ordained early and spent his years ministering in various communities while William entered the ministry later. In 1849 when they left Boston, both had been ordained.

The trip was very hard, and many storms were encountered. But the change from the frosts and storms of New England to the warm, dry clear weather of the tropics was enchanting. The *Forest* cast anchor in beautiful San Francisco harbor July 7, 1849.

"As we gazed upon the shore from the ship, nothing but a city of tents could be seen. Before leaving the vessel, the Captain called us on deck to have a friendly chat before bidding each other farewell and separating on our various ways. Arriving on shore, we found but five American families in the city, the balance being Mexican or Indians. We remained in the City [Editor's note: "City" refers to the City of San Francisco] five days," stated W. W. Smith.

The City of San Francisco provided great opportunities, for carpenters were in great demand. The brothers agreed to go to work at a point about 50 miles from San Francisco, located at the mouth of the San Joaquin River and arrived at their destination New York of the Pacific (Pittsburg) aboard the schooner *Rialto*, July 11, 1849, exactly 6 months after leaving Boston.

Colonel J. D. Stevenson and Dr. William Parker had purchased part of the Los Medaños Grant from José Antonio Mesa, the original holder. He received this grant in 1839 under the Mexican Government land grants, which consisted of 8,890.26 acres. They set up the lumber, fixtures and other necessities to commence the building of a city.

W. W. Smith was engaged by these men to take charge and superintend the building of a house for the families, which at the time were living in a tent. Each brother was to receive $14 per day. The colonel had agreed to pay the passage of the two Smith families, or $75 toward it. He also agreed to find each a

William W. Smith, taken before 1850. The hand of his brother, Joseph P. who died in February 1850, is seen resting on his right shoulder.

tenement for the first 6 months, rent free, and if they decided to stay in New York of the Pacific, give each a lot on which to build.

"Mr. Beemer and Antonio Mesa and family lived 2 miles further up the river. Mr. Mesa's house was built of split redwood logs, stood on end for the sides, and was covered with tules [Editor's note: Tules or Tule Rush (Schoenoplectus acutus var. occidentalis) is a native grass that grows in northern, southern and central California. It tends to grow in marshes and wet places, at elevations from 0–8,200 feet] in bundles for a roof, with a hole in the center to allow the smoke to escape, and contained two rooms," commented W. W. Smith.

The brothers commenced work July 13, and soon completed the New York House where they lived until they acquired it by purchase. They soon took in boarders at $16 per week. They also had a good number of guests who paid $1.25 per meal. The price of bread and beef was high. Butter and fruit were sometimes added to vary the menu. During the rainy season, the men, plying the river by boat, were glad to pay $1 a night to sleep on the floor in their own blankets. New York House became the popular temperance eating place.

Hearing of the arrival of W. W. and J. H. Smith, Dr. John Marsh came down to greet them and offer the hospitality of his home which lay 15 miles away. The party departed on horses provided by the doctor and shortly entered,

> ...a well beaten trail that led up the creek to the doctor's house. We found the doctor enjoying a siesta, stretched at full length upon the hairy side of a dry hide, in the grove back of the house, adjoining his vineyards. The doctor gave us a hearty welcome, and took us into his house made of adobe, and containing four rooms; he had not dishes enough to set the table for us; it was then the custom to roast the meat upon sticks before the fire, and to bake bread in the ashes.

During the visit with Dr. Marsh, the Smith brothers first saw and walked across the land that is now Antioch. On July 19, 1849, the brothers jointly took possession of 2 quarter-sections of land. One section upon which Antioch is now situated, the other upon which W. W. Smith resided. They worked the sections enough to hold them and also cut large quantities of firewood from them, but continued their labors at New York of the Pacific.

The land, now Antioch, had first been seen and used by the Indians [Editor's note: Indigenous People]. These first inhabitants were described by John Marsh and others as being of small stature "with broad shoulders, great strength and thought to be of the Bolgones [Editor's note: Present-day language group Bay Miwok] tribe. They possessed the same basic characteristics, customs and habits of Indian tribes found throughout California."

They constructed huts from boughs of trees, and evidence has been found of their temescal or "sweat-house". Most of the year they wore no clothing, and in the winter were half protected by skins from wild animals. They were thought to be a low form of Indian and at best, these Indians were considered inferior to the other Indians of North America.

The Indians around Antioch hunted for and ate mostly wild roots, including soap root. They dug small animals out of their holes. They ate earthworms and used flatworms as a spread for their bread made from acorns or crushed buckeye kernels. Grasshoppers were also a delicacy. At times, they would have deer, rabbit and game birds, wild fruits and berries. They probably had plenty of elk to eat, for Captain Kimball reported that he saw a herd of 80 or more elk the first morning after his arrival in Antioch, just outside his camp and that he shot a fine one of perhaps 400 pounds. During the first years, much of the meat which the settlers ate was elk, fresh or dried.

Herds grazed on the tule land and the islands across the San Juaquin River from Antioch. Deer were also plentiful, particularly in spots not often frequented by horsemen. They were often seen feeding on the bunch grass around Mt. Diablo. Antelope were also numerous. One antelope larger than the rest, was often seen by early settlers watching while the main body of antelope kids were at water, or on the bottom lands feeding on green grass. Antelope were good swimmers and often visited the islands of the river for green food.

The Indians of Northern California suffered greatly from two epidemics, cholera in 1833, and smallpox in 1838. Their numbers were greatly decreased.

In April 1869, when on excursion, W. W. Smith accompanied by his sons, Joseph and Charles, discovered an Indian burial ground on the part of the land immediately adjoining the Point. They dug up many flint arrow heads, shell ornaments and bone wampum.

Don Pedro Fages with his party, first saw Mt. Diablo and the great delta of the San Joaquin and Sacramento rivers from the highest hills of what is now Willow Pass on March 30, 1772. His party crossed to the present Kirker Creek and camped slightly east of present-day Antioch, and recrossed the range of hills south of Antioch the next day.

March 30, 1776, Father Crespi crossed the San Joaquin River not far from Antioch. In the summer of 1776, General M. G. Vallejo's father with Captain Rivera, traveled inland as far as the San Joaquin and reached an area that later became the Marsh ranch.

A surveying and exploring party under Sergeant José Antonio Sanchez, found fishing on the "Islands" across from present Antioch, excellent in October 1811. So states the diary of Ramon Abella, member of the party.

December 24, 1849, the Smith brothers erected tents and broke ground under the beautiful oaks, where now stands the town of Antioch. It was under these oaks that Joseph H. Smith was buried after his death, February 5, 1850. He had been weakened by the sea voyage and died of a lingering illness, "chills and fever" known as malaria fever. W. W. Smith leased the New York House to his brother's widow, Sarah B., and moved to his farm near Antioch. Antioch, at this time, was known as Smith's Point or the Point. These are located about a half-mile east of the original Antioch proper.

In the spring of 1850, while on a journey from Santa Clara, Mr. Smith met two brothers, Deacon John Pulsifer and Dr. Joseph Pulsifer, who were seeking land on which to settle. W. W. Smith told them of the land and space along the San Joaquin. He invited them to accompany him. Upon their arrival here, they made a trip around the tules and decided to erect a cabin. They laid out a garden on a flat above the Point, and when the rains commenced, they began to plow and plant. They constructed a windmill and pump to provide for the dry season. They cultivated one of the finest gardens within 10 miles during 1851–52, watering it by means of a wooden pump fixed in the slough. All hands helped build a fence and dig a ditch from the eastern to western tules in 1851, to keep stray animals away from the settlement.

September 1850, Reverend Smith heard of the arrival of a shipload of would-be settlers in San Francisco. Upon his arrival in San Francisco, he found a number of families who wished to obtain land. We invited them to settle at Smith's landing, and they accepted. These settlers were Captain George W. Kimball, a brother S. P. Kimball, four or five Hathaways, Mr. Marshall and son Benjamin, Mr. Robert Douglass and Mr. Dennison. Arriving at Smith's Landing, they laid out a street running east and west by compass and each family wishing land was presented with a lot upon which to build, by Mr. Smith.

Captain George Washington Kimball at age 73 said,

> I was born in Hancock County, Maine, October 10, 1805, on one of the 365 islands in Penobcot Bay. Farming and fishing was [Editor's note: *sic*] the business of my youth. School privileges were limited, but at the age of 18, I taught school in my own district, and after that I went on the water in the summer, and I went to an Academy or taught school in the winter. I dwell upon these school scenes with satisfaction, because they laid the foundation of a great event in my life and paved the way for me and over 200 other needy persons to find a home in the best country I ever saw, where hard times for industrious people have never yet come."

Carman Home 1866, corner of G Street between First and Second streets, stood for many years behind the hardware store and then the Famous Fashion Store. The above scene was at the wedding of their daughter.

The island of G. W. Kimball's birth was Kimball Island, which is part of the town of Isle au Haut. It is composed of the following islands: Isle au Haut, the two Spoon, York's, Fog, Burt, Merchant's, Kimball and all other islands south of Merchant's row. Hancock County was annexed to Knox County, by an act of the legislature, March 12, 1913.

Kimball ran a packet between Hain and New York in 1848, and on his last trip he decided to go to California. He conceived a plan for building a ship to carry poor people like himself. The following agreement resulted:

> We the undersigned, are desirous of engaging in an enterprise on the golden shores of California, the Paradise of America, where summer reigns perpetually; while fertile soil is yielding its increase abundantly, fruit growing spontaneously, fishes sporting most plentifully and where wild game is most prolific on the shores of the Pacific. Our object is to settle a township, or effect a permanent settlement on the coast of California, at some central point, in some capacious and commodious harbor, where the salubrity of the climate, the fertility of the soil, mill privileges, timber for shipbuilding, and other purposes, conveniences for fisheries, for coasting and other natural advantages, shall warrant a healthy and rapid settlement. For the accomplishment of the above-mentioned

object, we appoint George W. Kimball of Frankfort, County of Waldo, State of Maine, as our lawful agent, to purchase or build, man and equip, a ship suitable to perform said voyage to California; said ship to be ready for sea by the tenth day of October, 1849. From two to three hundred of us will build and own a fine packet of six hundred tons by paying one hundred and one dollars each; this packet will make one voyage per annum from Maine to California, taking out passengers, produce, etc. and returning with the exports of the Pacific. We will take our families, farming utensils, tools for the mechanic and apparatus for a sawmill. On our arrival the first object will be to select a township; second build a sawmill; erect a public depot for our families and baggage, until private dwellings can be built. When the packet sails, a school will commence for all on board, where the art of reading, writing, arithmetic, navigation, surveying and such branches of natural science will be taught as will be most needed in the new settlement.

Captain Kimball often remarked, "The boys on the coast of Maine tumble out of their cradles into a boat."

About six of the carpenters went into the woods, cut timber, and then helped build their own ship. Robert Douglass, a carpenter, commenced laying the ship's keel about the first of April, 1849, at Cutler. He worked alone the first week, but soon all of the 65 men were working on this ship. On November 11, the ship, partly rigged, sailed for Boston. It was 600 tons. (Though) the enterprise was a novelty, it was freely advertised by newspapers; merchants contributed freight and became interested in sending the vessel supplied with all needed ship chandlery.

March 4, 1850, they set sail for California with 300 persons aboard the *California Packet*. The trip was quite uneventful and pleasant. They arrived at San Francisco, where they found many were sick, and a few had died. All passengers of the *California Packet* arrived in good health, [Editor's note: It is unclear who arrived sick and who arrived healthy.] all from Boston with the three marines who swam out and boarded the ship at Rio de Janeiro and the 14 passengers who came aboard at Valparaiso, there was a total of 217 men, women and children, August 24, 1850. In San Francisco the company soon scattered, many going to the gold mines. Captain Kimball sold the ship to the South Sea Island Trader. It was wrecked in the South Seas not long after. He paid his bills and sat down to rest.

About September 12, 1850, Rev. W. W. Smith went aboard the ship and invited the remaining people to settle in the area now Antioch. It was then called New York Township. The group accepted the invitation of Rev. Smith and moved to Antioch, landing September 16, 1850, at the foot of Kimball (F) Street and built houses. The Captain Kimball House was the most westerly and the five other homes were built east to about where the now water tower of the 1940s stood at the corner of Sixth and A streets. The W. W. Smith house was larger than the others, built on a bluff overlooking the river.

Captain Mitchell, a mariner, living a bit east of Antioch, gave the people the galley from his ship to be used as a

Back of store operated by Mr. Klengel, brother of Otto Klengel, corner of 4th Street.

schoolhouse. It was moved to the block where the present Muir School stands. Miss Martha Douglass was installed as teacher, but because of ill health soon resigned, and Mr. Smith turned the school over to Adelia Barrett Kimball, daughter of Captain Kimball. She was 12-years-old. Adelia taught the school of half a dozen children a few months at a time for several years. The pupils were Edgar Kimball, Sarah Smith, Maria Mitchel, one or two Mitchel boys, two Douglass's and Ben Marshall. Adelia Kimball was the first permanent teacher of Antioch. She states,

> The house was small and dark, the out-of-doors big and bright. We had five recesses. The books we used were those the various families brought from the East. In those days we had no California State Series. The furniture was anything handy, a chair from home, or a rock if nothing else was available, the boxes were used for desks.

Adelia B. Kimball who later became Mrs. John Schott.

Soon after their arrival, cholera in its worst type broke out. The 5-year-old daughter, Sarah, of W. W. Smith recovered while many among them died, such as the Hathaway father, two sons, and wife of the eldest brother. The epidemic disappeared as mysteriously as it had appeared, leaving one or more invalids in every household. It was noted that those recovering from the epidemic were given the water submerge treatment during their spasms, given warm water enema and when conscious warm water to drink. None of those treated with medicine recovered, according to the knowledge of W. W. Smith.

Antioch survived the 1863 smallpox and typhoid fever epidemic of 1877.

John C. O'Brien arrived in Antioch late in 1850, to begin farming and other pursuits.

On July 4, 1851 a basket picnic was held at the residence of W. W. Smith, which stood on Wyatt Street, now Second Street near where the *Ledger* office in later years first stood, on the north side between Boobar and Galloway (G and H) streets.

The principle topic of the day, discussed by the group of between 30 and 40 men, women and children was, "What shall we name our town?" A chairman was chosen and several names were proposed, among them "Minton," after a steamer that ran up and down the river, in hopes that the steamer might be induced to stop at the landing. Another proposed name was "Paradise," but Deacon Pulsifer arose and said that there were many claimants to the lands of California, and they might lose their lands and it would then be "Paradise Lost." W. W. Smith then proposed that in as much as the first settlers were disciples of Christ, and one of them (his brother, Rev. Joseph H. Smith) had died and was buried on the land, it be given a Biblical name in his honor. He suggested "Antioch" after the Syrian city. No one by Smith had any special choice for a name, so he had little difficulty in persuading the people to christen the little town "Antioch" by united acclamation. W. W. Smith quoted, "The disciples were called Christians first in Antioch."

There were twelve towns in the United States named Antioch. Today, Antioch, California is the largest and most important of the twelve. [Editor's note: In 1971].

The year 1851 was very dry. All vegetation was blighted. The Antioch residents had to go as far as Diablo Valley to cut hay and transport it to their homes by way of [Editor's note: 5 or 6 words illegible in original photostatic printing], the settlers found plenty of hay in the foothills and valleys, which were covered with wild oats. The tule land produced an abundance of course grass. The hay did not give a sufficient income for the entire year, though it was taken by scow to San Francisco where it was sold for $60 per ton. This enterprise was carried on by Captain Kimball and his brother, S. P. Kimball. The little band of settlers scattered, some taking their houses with them; other abandoning theirs entirely or temporarily, so that the later returned from the Antioch of 1852 was literally a deserted village. Captain Kimball later returned from the Kirker Pass region. McMasters came and built by the river front. James Henderson came in 1853. W. W. Smith returned and other families moved into the vicinity. There were no town limits. Henderson lived at the present Arata place; Thompson at March [sic Marsh] Landing; Madam Fuller at Oak Point. Wyatt came in 1852 and with O'Brien located southwest of the new present papermill. Robert Fuller in 1852 settled at the ranch of Dr. Adams at Oak Springs; and Hustels in the sandhills. There [sic] were the near neighbors of the Antioch family, the G. W. Kimballs.

D Street wharf on the river with Tom Gain's home to the left.

During the next few years, the growth was slow in the country, but Antioch kept up its progressive start. Each family vied with the other to make it a pleasant abode; charming unanimity in all their actions was the result. Each new family made an epoch in its history and was welcomed gladly. Some more of the earliest settlers were Charles V. Smith in 1853, William R. Forman in 1852, Ferdinand and Christian Hoffman (moved to Byron in 1861), William Newman in 1859, William Gilchrist and Andrew Portman in 1860.

House built by William R. Forman at First and F streets. This house stood on the bluff overlooking the river and the point where the first permanent settlers set foot in Antioch. Picture taken in 1951.

McKellips home picture left center. The old Catholic Church is located to the extreme right. The center house, first right was the Dunnigan house then the J. Rio Baker house. The other house was built by J. Rio Baker. Mount Diablo is in the upper right background.

An 1880s view of Antioch. In the right bottom, there is an engine of the coal railroad running down F Street, at the 5th Street intersection. The Congregational Church is shown center right. Bob Hale's house is located behind the church and Dr. Wemple's is shown beyond, to the south. The top of the Will's farmhouse can be seen. The Weldie house can be seen just below it.

During these early years, Reverend Smith was in and out of Antioch, working many places, helping to build many of the buildings in this part of the country. On Sundays, he would walk many miles to preach in the various tiny communities. Some of his favorite places were in the Mt. Diablo Township. Reverend Smith had united Dr. John Marsh and Miss Abigail Tuck in marriage June 24, 1851. She died in 1855, and in September 1856, Dr. Marsh was murdered by three drunken vaqueros as he drove toward Martinez. The Antioch home of his son, Charles Marsh, built in the 1880s, still stands on the southwest corner of Fourth and G streets.

The year 1853 was very important for Antioch, for it was then that W. W. Smith built a wharf on the slough west of town for the landing of steamers bringing the U.S. Mail. It was at the foot of Parsons (J) Street and in later years, was the favorite fishing spot of many.

The same year, the Fuller family acquired by purchase, the land occupied by Swain and Darby. Religious services were commenced in the residence of W. W. Smith and later continued in the Fuller home and others. James Henderson and his wife, Jane, started the business of butter and cheese making. She continued the business for a number of years. They moved to the "Tron House" where Mrs. Henderson died in 1862. In that year, J. C. McMasters and G. W. Kimball established a dairy business in Antioch after having been the first to grow wheat between Kirker Pass and Antioch in 1853. W. Lock had moved to Antioch that year and had built his home and planted trees west of town.

Money was very scarce and a pinch of gold dust would buy a drink of some of the acute necessities sent to Antioch from San Francisco. The only means of contact with the outside world was the schooner *Enterprise*, commanded by Captain Miller, with "Charley" as the crew. It made a weekly (delivery of) products of farm and dairy to the City, bringing back the numerous things needed by the community. The community had a feeling of gratitude and misery toward the trip." Gratitude for a means of transportation and kindness of the Captain and misery of the trip sometimes three days in length and the inevitable seasickness." This sentiment was related by Adelia Kimball, later Mrs. A. B. Schott, on one of her journeys to San Francsico to school or to teach sometime prior to June, 1863.

Antioch was completely dependent upon the river for its means of contact with any other community. There were no established roads, no railroads and no surrounding populated areas with which to trade. The river brought to Antioch the people, food, goods, and made possible agriculture and later industry, which kept Antioch advancing through the years.

Antioch was blessed with deep water facilities, second to none. Antioch was the States' furthest inland area where high land and deep water meet. Any ocean vessel entering the Golden Gate can travel the waterways to Antioch without trouble where the harbor is 40-feet deep, 3 miles of frontage, three-quarters of a mile wide.

Early in the 1850s, the first wharf was built by the pioneers. To San Francisco they sent grain and hay from the nearby areas and received in return foods not raised here, clothing, and building materials.

After the Gold Rush fever died down, Antioch began to be bypassed by the larger boats as they had no paying cargo. To take care of the situation, it was found that (with the) natural growth and establishment of the now Antioch Lumber Company, the problems were solved. The lumber company fed building materials into the surrounding areas and made Antioch a port of call for the lumber schooners for many years.

The social life of the first years was a monthly sewing bee with lunch, which met "turn about" [Editor's note: rotating host] at several neighbors, where they sewed for the hostess and exchanged news. There was an occasional traveling preacher and Sunday service, led by Reverend Smith.

Moving of furniture, lumber, fencing, and farm equipment was frequently done by an ox team. The team owned by Captain Kimball was oftentimes used. The teams were brought from New England to California possibly by vessel via Panama or around Cape Horn. Captain Kimball and his brother hired a man and cut hay on Kimball and Sherman islands.

The leading industry quickly became that of cattle raising. Dr. Marsh had large herds of wild Spanish cattle, and those who wished could have the use of a limited number of cattle and half the increase for breaking them. Had the milking qualities equaled the length of the horns and their athletic abilities, these cattle would have been very valuable. What little milk they did give was very rich, and proved a fair investment to those who chose to avail themselves of Dr. Marsh's offer.

The land grant problem was very thorny to the land owners of Antioch and the county. Clear titles were hampered by the Spanish grants which defied legally established boundaries for many years. These grants always seemed to include every fertile spot. Therefore, the grant of Dr. Marsh was not settled until 1862. The United States was slow in giving titles to lands in dispute. Antioch was on land claimed by New York, better known as Medaños, and Marsh grants. The people claiming land in Antioch were in and out of courts for many years, first gaining, then losing but always trying to get the government title to the land until a final settlement was made.

In the case of W. W. Smith, as early as 1854, he was surveying his eastern boundary in an effort to establish the line of the Marsh grant. In 1865, he built his house 37-feet east of the Township survey line. In February of 1866, he received notice of Galloway and Boobar that he was a trespasser. He went down to National Hall with Captain Kimball, but the hall was closed. They soon learned, while walking through the streets, that there were many riotous threats to tar and feather and pitch Parson Smith into the river. This constant friction continued to exist between Smith and those residents of Antioch who claimed the land on which he lived belonged to the Township. He moved to his 4-acre ranch, located along the railroad, between Pittsburg Landing and Somersville, about 2 miles below Somersville, where he remained for several years. However, he always referred to his farm on Sixth Street just east of A Street in Antioch as "home". In 1869, Smith made many trips to and from San Francisco over his land grant. In March, Judge Hoffman came up, with lawyers and reporters and examined the premises of the grant.

An early business of Antioch located at the corner of Second and G streets.

Smith wrote the Secretary of the Interior in Washington, D. C. several times concerning the grants. In November of 1869, Smith was in Sacramento with the registrar of the Land Office of San Francisco. The registrar and receiver took the testimony of Joseph and Charles Smith, sons of W. W. Smith, at their Antioch residence. The title was granted. Thursday, November 18, 1869, was the first day title ownership was enjoyed on their own land and was a day of real thanksgiving. Captain Kimball states,

Red Front Bar owned by M. S. Rodgers, father of Jak Rodgers. Shown are Mr. Rodgers and Mr. Fisher.

> I supposed I owned the section I live on until 1865, as I had bought all the titles I know of. Garcia told me his New York ranch did not reach me, but they finally located it over my place and covered my improvements and the courts said it was all right. After the New York grant took my land, I bought a few parcels of land to save some improvements. Then I fled to the tule island opposite Pittsburg Landing with my stock. I spent part of two seasons there, dairying and raising hogs. I also bought the little island (Kimball) opposite Antioch; from this island, my son, Edgar H. Kimball, supplies Antioch with milk.

During the years that Captain Kimball was in court about his land claims, he and his family lived on Kimball Island, and he carried on his various business enterprises from there.

In 1869, Captain Kimball spent much of his time in court at Martinez over his claims. The Los Medaños claim was given title in 1872. After this date, Captain Kimball bought back some of his original property. The original land he bought back was mainly the block including his home between Emmerson, Kimball, Brown and Marsh (E, F, Third and Fourth) streets.

An interesting case which developed out of the land grants was Wills vs. Robinson. The Wills ranch included land west of East (A) Street to the railroad and south to Rattan (Tenth) Street to the Southern Pacific tracks. In the middle 1860s, Manuel Peoche came to California supposedly authorized to purchase the land for a syndicate of Frenchmen. Some felt that he was dishonest and bought the Los Medaños grant for himself. He was connected with L. L. Robinson in business. When Peoche was found dead in his office, evidence was found from his papers that all the property was titled to Robinson. Whether the Los Medaños claim included Antioch at this time was the major dispute. Mr. Robinson claimed 40 percent of all the land in the Los Medaños grant or equal value of it. This meant anyone having purchased property from Mr. Wills now owed Mr. Robinson 40 percent of the value and the back rent. Mr. Robinson was not quite the blackguard he seemed, for he gave titles to the churches and to the school. He also made fair settlements with people not able to pay at the above rate. The case was in court for more than 7 years before it was settled in August 1885, in favor of Mr. Robinson.

[Editor's note: Handwritten receipt to Galloway & Boobar for real estate sale. Antioch March 10, 1864 signed by George W. Kimball.]

Antioch, lying between the Marsh and Los Medaños grants, had years of harassment and wearing litigation and was finally taken over by the Los Medaños grant. Galloway and Boobar then bought the town.

On March 12, 1864, Galloway and Boobar agreed to pay G. W. Kimball $1,000 for Block 13, now known as Block 8, between Front and Wyatt and Boobar and Galloway (First, Second, G and H) streets, to be paid as follows: $100 down, $400 in 30 days and $500 in 90 days. On the receipt of the last payment, Kimball agreed to give a "good and sufficient" deed for the property.

[Editor's note: Words missing] ...purchased the west half of section 13 and east half of section 28, embracing the town and what became Mr. Will's farm. They had the land laid out and surveyed by Mr. Eddy, later county surveyor, and it became known as the Eddy Survey. This Eddy Survey and one made by T. A. McMalon in 1884, became the official surveys of Antioch. The northern boundary of Antioch is the low-water line. The earliest survey of Antioch was made in 1862, by Wyatt and O'Brien, who entered the state tule land west of town, laying it out in blocks and lots west of Galloway (H) Street. Two companies among the first to build stores on this land were Wolf and Company and Kimball and Co.

The settlers learned very soon that by handling the soil properly, farming could be very successful and profitable. During the first decade, every known grain was produced; many fruit trees were planted, among them peach, plum, pear, apple, quince, and various nut trees and a large variety of vegetables were grown. Small fruits and vines were also successfully tried. Asparagus soon became very important and was first grown by the Biglows in the slough region east of town, the present Fulton Shipyard area. Other early growers of asparagus were George Upham and John Schott. The settlers also raised the small food fowls and animals. They depended to a great extent on the wild fowl of the islands.

Life on Sherman, Kimball and Winter islands was controlled largely by the wind and tide. When the weather was too windy and rough, the inhabitants of the islands remained at home regardless of plans. They reached the mainland by sailing or rowing. The description of the weather from day to day show that there has been oft-mentioned fog, wind, frost, "little rain", hot weather, and even occasional falling of snow in Antioch which reminds one of the unusual year 'round weather of today. The vegetables and fruits grown on the mainland were successfully grown on the islands. Asparagus was grown at an early date on Sherman and Kimball islands by Captain Kimball and his son, Edgar.

Residence, G. W. Kimball.

Antioch Ledger, Monday, March 20, 1972 - Page 5

Irish birth day for 88-year-old twins

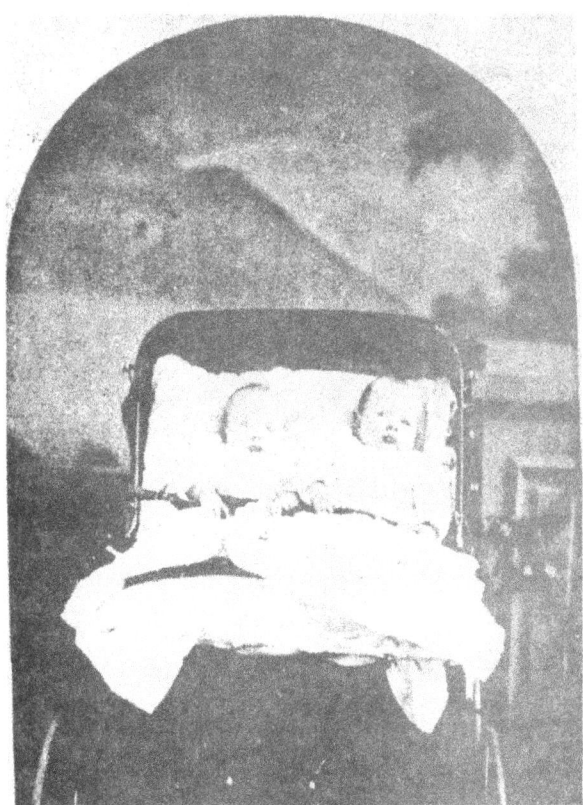

IDENTICAL TWINS - Carrie and Sadie Kimball, granddaughters of Captain George W. Kimball, Antioch's founding father, were born on March 16, 1884.

STILL GOING STRONG - Now Carrie Griswold and Sadie Wrinkle, the widowed twins, who still like dancing, quilting and bridge, and still dress alike, celebrated an Irish birthday party in Hayward.

Early lighting in the homes was by candles or whale oil lamps. The first kerosene lamp in Antioch was brought by Adelia Kimball to her mother, when she returned from school in San Francisco. It was cause for quite a bit of excitement among their neighbors.

Of interest anytime, are prices. The following are quoted from the store ledger of the Kimball store in 1864 and 1865, this store was located on the northwest corner of Galloway and Wyatt (Second and H) streets. The store was owned by G. W. Kimball but run by D. J. Peterson and E. H. Kimball for which they paid $15 rent per month to the senior Kimball.

2 bars soap, 25 cents
1/4 gallon oil, 50 cents
*1 sack salt, 25 cents
1 lb. butter, 25 cents
21/2 lbs. sugar, 50 cents
9 lbs. bacon, $2.25
2 lbs. crackers, 25 cents
*1 can lard, $2.25
*1 sack flour, $3.25
1 lb. tea, $1.00
6 lbs. coffee, $2.00
10 lbs. apples, $1.00
5 lbs. rice, 50 cents
1 box allspice, 25 cents
1 keg syrup, $4.00
1 lb. cream of tartar, 75 cents
20 lbs. potatoes, $1.00
1 dozen eggs, 25 cents
**other eggs, 75 cents

50 lbs. beans, $2.50
1 keg pickles, $2.00
1 lb. starch, 25 cents
13 lbs. cabbage, 32 cents
1 lb. saleratus, 15 cents
1 hair brush, 75 cents
1 curry comb, 50 cents
1 box axle grease, 63 cents
1 lantern, $1.00
1 plug tobacco, 50 cents
1 pair boots, $4.00
1 pair socks, 50 cents
1 lb. candles, 25 cents
10 lbs. nails, 75 cents
1 broom, 50 cents
1 can paint, 38 cents
1 box pain killer, 25 cents
1 pair gloves, $1.50
3 pairs stockings, $1.50

1 wash board, 38 cents
2 yards denim, 90 cents
1 can white lead, $2.50
1/2 gal. turpentine, $1.50
1 knife, 38 cents
1 handkerchief, $1.00
1 pair shoes, $1.25
1 lbs. shot, $2.00
1 bottle ink, 50 cents
1 pair pants, $3.00
1 vest, $4.00
1 hatchet, 80 cents
1 skirt, $2.00
1 pair drawers, $2.00
2 shirts, $2.50
1 ball wicking, 10 cents
1 bottle castor oil, 25 cents

*No mention is made as to the weight of the salt, lard or flour.
**No reference is made to the type of eggs.

Kimball General Store at the northwest corner of Second and H streets, as seen in 1937 and 1970.

The first post office in this district was at New York of the Pacific, officially called Junction. In 1852, the name was changed and the office moved to Antioch, on Wyatt (Second) between Galloway and Main (H and I) streets. G. W. Kimball was appointed postmaster. During his visit to the mines, J.C. McMasters was deputed to attend to the duties of the office and was succeeded by Mr. Eddy.

September 10, 1864, Antioch held a public meeting with Charles P. Marsh [Editor's note: Son of Dr. John Marsh] acting as chairman, where a resolution, promising the hearty cooperation of the citizens in a railroad project, mainly to please J.C. McMaster, connecting Oakland and Antioch and San Joaquin Valley railroad.

It was to run through the hills east and south of Antioch. Eddy, Smith, Kimball, T. O. Carter, Tregallus, James Boobar, Benjamin Smith and Herbert Stichfield were present. "Rough places for a railroad," was a comment of Smith. Much time was spent by the organizers but to no success. The first railroad was not to come through Antioch until September 9, 1875. It was the San Pablo and Tulare, now the Southern Pacific Railroad.

After the first few hard years, W. W. Smith and his family left Antioch in 1855 to travel around the county from place to place as he found carpentry work. In July 1862, Smith entered the U.S. Navy and served for 6 months on the U.S. Flagship *Lancaster*. He settled mainly in Antioch but helped build most of the buildings in this part of the county for the next 20 years. The Smiths lost three of their early children, all of them dying before 6 months, and the doctor later discovered that it was malnutrition from unwholesome mother's milk. The last two children, Charles L. and James F., survived as they received cow's milk from nursing bottles. His other children to live were William M., by his first wife, Sarah L., and Joseph L., by the second marriage. The W. W. Smith house was the first house built in the township. It was later moved to the site of the old Antioch Hospital, Utter (Sixth) Street, east of East (A) Street. County taxes on the Smith "home" in 1879, were $48.10. In fact, one of the houses comprising the old hospital was built by W. W. Smith's son, Charles. The original home was torn down after 1900. It was constructed of lumber brought from Brazil. The siding boards were wide and long, of mahogany. It was torn down by a lumber company for the valuable lumber.

W. W. Smith was liberal in his religious beliefs and never dogmatic, believing in the Gospel of Love. He loved to sing. He believed in the prohibition of liquor traffic and in woman suffrage. Mrs. Smith passed away in September 1899, and 3 weeks later, he joined her at the age of 88. They are both buried in the family plot just to the right of the main gate of the Free Masons and Odd Fellow Cemetery (Oak View). George W. Kimball mentions, "W. W. Smith moved from Antioch, so that I am the first permanent settler. I built two small wharves for receiving coal. I was the first postmaster, the first notary public, the first justice of the peace and the first school trustee in Antioch."

Captain Kimball was one of the best-known pioneer residents of Contra Costa County. He died November 18, 1879, at the age of 74. He had been a resident since September 16, 1850. He was known as a man of generous and human feelings, marked intellectuality, originality and independence of thought. Through his efforts, Antioch was helped on its way to a prosperous town, well planned and sanely governed. He was always helping the needy and giving to the churches. He is buried in the family plat to the far left of the main gate of the Free Masons and Odd Fellows Cemetery. His wife, Caroline Barrett Kimball, died December 10, 1897. Their home was built on the site just east of the later Scouts Hall, located at Brown and Kimball (Third and F) streets. It was the only house of the original group left standing until after the 1950s. It was the oldest house in Antioch and thought to be the oldest used residential building in the county. Some of the material of the house was brought from Maine on the initial voyage of the captain's good ship. Captain Kimball cut and hauled hay by scow to San Francisco where he traded it for Oregon lumber from which his house was built. In the 1870s, there were three houses in a row on Brown (Third) Street, Kimball's to the west, a Greek family by the name of Psyche, and further east, the home of Kemer Blanchard.

Adjoining the Kimball's main house structure on the east was a single room with an earthen floor, entered by way of a homemade door fastened by a finger latch. The original house was "a lovely two-story New England-type home, white with green shutters and a large front porch". The house was later remodeled by Mr. Griswold and remained in the form until it was torn down in 1956. Mr. Griswold had married Kimball's granddaughter, Caroline Kimball. The first twins born in Antioch were Caroline and Sarah Kimball, March 17, 1884.

The old burial ground known as "God's Acres" was north of Rattan (Tenth) Street and extended west of Kimball (F) Street for two blocks. It soon proved to be too small. A company was formed by the Free Masons and Odd Fellows and a tract of land selected among the live oaks, two-and-one-half miles east of Antioch. It is the present cemetery. As quickly as possible in 1882, those buried within the town limits were exhumed and removed to the new location.

Reverend Smith drew the bridge plans for the county during 1872 and helped build some of the bridges. He worked on the Galloway wharf the same year. Most of the early wharves were built for private use and were small and later replaced by the large wharves for general use. The first wharf was built by Smith in 1853, to be used for the landing of the U.S. mail. It was later used for shipping coal, before the railroad on Kimball (F) Street was built and was known as the Levy Wharf and later the Municipal Wharf located at the foot of Parsons (J) Street. By 1880, it was not in use for shipping but became the fisherman's paradise. Kimball built several wharves for the shipping of coal after 1860, and by 1865,

Unidentified Landscape

Unidentified Landscape. Possibly the Jost Distillery Company wharf.

Smith had added another wharf for the shipping of wood near the Point. In 1859, Galloway built his first wharf later to become one of the Grange wharves at the foot of Emmerson (E) Street, connected to [Editor's note: Sic. another wharf located] at the foot of Vanderwater (D) Street, which the Grange had built in 1871 by Galloway and Boobar. The Antioch Distillery Co. built its own private wharf at the foot of East (A) Street. A wharf at the foot of Kimball (F) Street, was constructed for the use of shipping coal with the completion of the coal railroad in 1878. The last of the large wharves built by the now Antioch Lumber Company was the City Wharf at the foot of Galloway (H) Street extending over to Main (I) Street, known now as the Riverview.

An improvement to serve Antioch was the building of dikes to protect the tule land on the mainland and the fertile soil of the islands from the overflow of the river during high tide season.

Two Grange associations were started in the township in 1864, one at Antioch, the other at Point of Timber. Antioch Grange purchased a wharf and fixtures from Mr. Boobar, paying $10,600.

They divided the land accompanying it into small lots to suit the buyers, thus hoping to liquidate the debt. They built a good hall (Antioch Lumber Co. office building), but by 1882, the Antioch Grange had failed and was defunct property without value. In 1871, the Grange Corporation contracted to build a wharf at the foot of Vanderwater (D) Street, cost to be $7,000. In June 1874, Captain Kimball was elected president of the Grange Corporation with William Sellers as secretary and Mrs. T. Wills, treasurer. In spite of hard work by the interested members, the grange continued to fail in operations, and by 1879 many were in favor of closing up the business of the wharf and warehouse. The need to close had been realized by some before 3 years had passed. The Grange Hall had a meeting place on the second floor with store facilities on the first floor.

Original City Hall and Jail, located at Third Street between G and H on the north side of the street.

Fires during the first years held more than the usual terror for the town. In October 1864, the home of Dr. J. P. Howard, with all its papers, valuables, personal effects and furnishings was completely destroyed. Early one Sunday, August 23, 1871, a fire broke out on Main (I) Street, in a wash house of the Griffin Hotel (American Exchange), at the southeast corner of Main and Wyatt (I and Second) streets. A north wind was blowing with great violence at the time. At that hour, the inhabitants of course, were asleep, and the fire was well ahead before it was discovered. The timber was very dry, and with the wind, it raised a running mountain of fire, appalling the hearts of the suddenly awakened sleepers. In a few minutes after discovery, the fire leaped on to and enveloped Chase & Robbins Livery Stable, filled with hay on the northeast corner of Main and Brown (I and Third) streets. It made a wild sweep to the opposite corner and took in McCoy's two-story shop, then his home in the rear. It continued south to envelope D. Cleaver's home, a vacant house where Knapp once lived, which was at the extreme south of the second block from where the fire had started. Here, the fire slowly lulled in calm of exhaustion. Not more than 40 minutes had elapsed until all of these buildings were razed. In the meantime, the fire extended north to Griffin's two-story lodging house at a slower pace, but no less final in its efforts. From here, the fire soon caught the main hotel building, which was two stories high, about 70-feet by 70-feet and elevated in location, in and a little above the most dense [Editor's note: sic] portion of the town. Those viewing the grand and awful scene said it had the brightness of a noon day sun at two o'clock in the morning. The fire spread east from the hotel to McCartney's home next door, then their variety story, then Tapperner's Shoe Store, then Hop Lee's wash-house, which the townsmen tore down to save other buildings. Here, in a torn-down building, the monster called a truce and slept upon his laurels of three blocks of the town in smoke and ashes. Six places of business and four dwellings were gone when the flames died away. Eighteen thousand dollars' worth of property was destroyed, upon which there was about $10,000 insurance.

Before the fire, several Chinese stores and dwellings including Hop Lee's were located on Wyatt (Second) Street. Hop Lee advertised in the weekly newspaper, the Antioch *Ledger*, "Wash-house clothes are not beaten to pieces, nor does he send home linen without sewing on the buttons."

Antioch City Hall, built in 1926 and located at Third and H streets.

When rebuilt, Hop Lee's wash-house was on Front (First) Street between Boobar and Galloway (G and H) streets, later torn down for the lumber warehouse. Most of the Chinese homes, comprising Antioch's Chinatown, were located on both sides of Front (First) Street between Galloway and Main (H and I) streets and on the east side of Main (I) Street from Front to Wyatt (First to Second) streets.

The *Ledger* was established by J. E. Townsend and Harry Waite with its first issue circulated March 10, 1870 (Editor's note: date unclear], as a letter, 4 x 6-inches. This was the first bit of local printing. The first newspaper issue was March 26, 1870, and became the second-oldest paper in the county. The office was first located about where the Ward Law offices are today. The paper came out every Saturday. The price was $4.00 per year or $2.50 for 6 months, strictly in advance. Since the first issue, the paper has never failed to go to print.

Ledger Newspaper Building after 1882, located south of G Street on Third, where PG&E is situated today. C. F. Montgomery was editor. His home is on the left.

In August 1870, Townsend became the sole owner. In December of the same year, J. P. Abbot bought a half interest. Townsend sold the other half to E. G. Fuller, who sold it to H. A. Weaver in 1872. In 1873, Abbott became the sole owner and editor. He carried the paper until 1881 when he leased it to C. H. Smith.

Abbott was interested in politics and was elected state senator from the 11th Senatorial District (Marin and Contra Costa counties) in 1886.

In 1882, Charles F. Montgomery became the owner, and after his death, his son, Curtis F. Montgomery, was in charge until April 1905 when F. McDaniel bought the paper. In 1921, A. Flaherty became the owner. In the 1880s the *Ledger* moved its office to the other side of Wyatt (Second) Street and east a block where PG & E now stands. November 4, 1929, the *Ledger* became a tri-weekly. The records of the Board of Supervisors of Contra Costa County show the petition for the incorporation of the town of Antioch under the date of February 6, 1872. The document and the names signed, follow:

> We the undersigned (being the majority of the Town of Antioch, and qualified electors and residents thereof for more than 30 days last past, the said town containing more than 200 inhabitants), do now most respectfully petition Your Honorable Body to incorporate the said town, under the name of Antioch, the same being about one mile in width by about three miles in length (but not exceeding the same), and situated on the San Joaquin River, adjoining the New York grant in this county, as per plate or map hereto attached; said town to be incorporated for police purposes, and other purposes. Pursuant to the statutes of this state. And your petitioners will ever pray, etc.
>
> *M. Donlon, Joseph Galloway, M. A. Morrisey, Cyrus Cheney, William Jones, Oliver Wolcott, H. Gardner, M.S. Levy, W. Rountree, J.C. McMaster, Charles Kohn, S. Franklin Pitts, J. T. Cossan, Van W. Phillips, Joseph Ott, Robert West, F. Wilkening, James Martin, G. B. Robins, William C. Johnson, James Ewing, Frederick Vollmer, Henry N. Baker, Charles Peers, Ferdinand Stain, W. A. Brunkhorst,*

George Thyarks, James Conroy, George Gruenwald, Albert Brink, G. W. Kimball, T. N. Wills, J. J. McNulty, H.W. Fassett, George Miller, G. S. Carman, R. B. Hard, Stephen Jessup, Francis Williams, Abraham Low, Stephen Abbott, Job E. Warren, T. O. Carter, Jay Tuttle, George McCoy, J. A. Chittenden, George W. Brown, A. M. Marble, H. B. Reed, J. P. Abbott, Jospeh Baules, E. J. Fuller, James Gard, John Tappeinen, G. E. Wright, I. Lobree, Charles Wein, D. McCartney, Joseph Sheirwelup, J. R. Howard, H. Rietoro, Oscar M. Jessup, H. L. Farland, P. Griffin, J. H. Lewis, A. Brown, S. T. Page, H. W. Brewer, Joseph L. Smith, R. R. Fuller, Peter Donlan, Christian Humble, Frank McFarlane, George A. Swain, H.A. Foster, P. McDermott, H. Williamson, H. Seers, D. Mayon, H. H. Dearien, D. N. Cleaves, J. E. Bollinger, R. J. Wally, R. G. Houston, James T. Cushing, John W. Strickler, George Perry, S. S. Pitts, J. Nicholson, M. H. Jacobs, T. Aug. Heinoch, John B. Turner, Thomas Martin, R. Taylor, S. B. Joslin, Warren Abbott, D. P. Mahan, M. Homburg, P. Strickfield, Joseph P. Barron.

The first meeting of the Board of Trustees of the new incorporated town, was held March 2, 1872. R. B. Hard became chairman, and the other members were T. N. Wills, James Ewing, J. C. McMaster and George Gruenwald. M.S. Levy became clerk. Bonds of the Marshall, Assessor and Treasurer were set at $1,000 each. On March 4 of the same year, the by-laws were passed. Ordinance No. 1 prohibited owners of stock to suffer the same to run at large within the limit of the town.

An ordinance was passed regulating the use of firearms. Mr. Hard was elected president, and a motion was passed to have him instructed to furnish and repair the town prison. The following day, a town ordinance regulated the use of defective flues on stoves. The bonds of the three officers were approved. Petition of the citizens to the Board praying [sic] that a certain "dog-crib" be exempt from taxation. License tax for all carrying on business within the limits of Antioch was set at $3.50. A discussion on the repair of the streets, followed. A committee of three was appointed to investigate.

The original Belshaw Store. It was torn down and replaced by the later Belshaw Store and Theater. The building still stands at Second and G streets (the Masonic Hall). Pictured from left are John Doulan (on the truck), Jay and John Belshaw, Frank Wills, ed Rapp and Will Purchase.

The boundaries of the incorporated town of Antioch in 1872 were: North - low water of the San Joaquin River; East - the present A Street; South - the present Tenth Street; West - the present O Street.

The first annexation of land to Antioch was a piece of land 360-feet deep, south of Tenth Street between G and L streets.

The following ordinances give some other actions of the Board of Trustees of Antioch:

Ordinance No. 3 (still on the books): Fines will be assessed for those creating a nuisance by littering the streets.

Ordinance No. 9: "any board member not present at roll call at a regular or called meeting of the board without a lawful excuse therefore shall be fined $1 for each offense. And in order to secure the attendance of absent member of the board shall have the power to order the marshal to arrest the absentees and bring them to the board."

Whether this section was ever used is not noted but there are many records of board members carefully asking permission to absent themselves.

The Tyler Hotel, made of Antioch brick, stood on I between First and Second streets. The building still stands as part of Marquetti's.

Ordinance No. 4: "It is unlawful to deposit hot ashes in any wooden vessel or in any vacant lot or premises, unless the same shall have first been thoroughly saturated with water.

Surprised? This was still on the books in 1951.

Ordinance No. 26, May 7, 1877: "A 5 mph speed limit on the first railroad planned to operate though the city."

Ordinance No. 33: practically forbade anyone even to look in the direction of an opium smoker on fear of a fine "not over $100." Opium smoking had become quite a community problem due to the influx of coolie labor [Editor's note: Chinese labor] of the 1870s and 1880s.

An 1883 Ordinance compelled the town marshal to inspect every building in the city twice a year in the interest of finding and eliminating fire hazards. The hazards found had to be eliminated in 10 days or the city did the work, and a lien was charged against the property.

Ordinance: "no one may disturb the peace by driving or riding horses through the streets at an immoderate or unusual gait or rate of speed."

The first business licensing ordinance exempted from tax those selling articles they manufactured themselves or foodstuffs they raised themselves. This ordinance also "prescribed licenses for the saloons that furnished drinks in quantities of one quart or more," soon amended to "to provide a license for the less-than-one-quart establishments that was higher than the over-a-quart rate."

A southeast view of Antioch from Sixth and G streets about 1890. Worrell home is shown in the lower left, and the J. Rio Baker home is shown with the Dunnigan home to the west.

An ordinance dealing with children stated that children under 16 had to be off the streets before 9 p.m. There were no objections to getting up at 5 a.m. to help with the chores around home, place of business or the farm. Failing to comply brought fines of $1.00 to $20.00 and up to 20 days in jail or both.

Children were also forbidden to spin their tops on the sidewalks, or ride their bicycles, tricycles, velocipedes or "so-called safetys" [Editor's note: A 'safety' bicycle was any bicycle that attempted to seat the rider nearer the ground than they could on an 'Ordinary' high bicycle. For example, today's "recumbent" bicycle] thereon.

The first water rate ordinance in 1905 set a monthly charge of $1.00 for a family of five or less, added 10 cents a month for each additional person and another 25 cents if the family had a "patent water closet". If the water closet was open to the public use, the charge was 40 cents.

An ordinance of 1912, regulation of saloons, set hours from 5 a.m. to 1 a.m. but prohibited music or singing after 10 p.m. on weekdays and not at all on Sundays. This lasted until Prohibition.

Ordinance No. 117-A, 1933 read: Young people under 18 years of age are breaking the law if they attend a public dance without the company of a parent, guardian or adult having custody over them. Dancing cannot start before 9 p.m. and must end by 3 a.m.

In 1883, an ordinance required fireproofing of stove flues and those of other heating devices and provided for inspection by the marshal twice a year. Was this the first of our building and zoning laws?

Politics entered the board early, and all five members faced election every year. Early in 1873, only one of the original five members faced election every year. Early in 1873, only one of the original five was returned. In the fall of the same year, two members, J. F. Abbott and T. N. Wills, resigned, and after the second election, ex-trustees R. B. Hard and G. W. Brown became members. The first action of the new Board at the request of Mr. Hard, was to confront ex-trustee Wills before the board, "to show cause why the assessment of his property should not be higher. "It is noted that later the assessment was boosted $2,000."

There were battles over street improvements, location of the streets and the amount of work to be done. But then as now, property owners paid for the improvements through formation of a simple assessment district.

The streets of Antioch for many years were dust bowls in the dry season and sloughs of mud in the wet season. There was an emulsion of oil test paving installed on Second Street which apparently was "just a mass of water-filled, muddy chuckholes. "In 1914, under the Street Improvement Act of 1911, 47 blocks of oil macadam were put in at a cost of $84,000. In 1916–17, 54 blocks of concrete base and 1½-inches of Topeka Top were laid for $120,000.

In 1912, the original street names such as Manhatten, Galloway, Wyatt, and Marsh to name a few, were changed to our present system of letters and numbers.

On May 2, 1872, Thomas Sutton was named as nightwatchman supplementing day policeman James Cushing. The minutes show a request to hire William Long as night watchman as soon as a vacancy occurs. A later entry showed "Sutton fired,

Antioch's Second Street about 1890, looking west from the south side of G Street. Pictured from left to right: S. Josleu's Harness Shop and House Barber Shop, O'Brien Hall - top floor, Baker and George Drug Store, Main floor, North side, right to left: Palace Hotel, Store and Printing Office, Bank, Frank Wills' house, Robert Wall Shoe Store, and Arlington Hotel. The first man on the left is Mr. Treugrove.

Long hired." This kept up until Long was discharged and Sutton reappointed in June, 1875. The appointment was rescinded the next day because allegedly he was not a United States citizen. Fred Wilkening got the job, and a year later, there was brisk mention that J. W. Jones was appointed night watchman, but no mention was made of what happened to Wilkening. It was noted that in 1890, Antioch's population was 1,200.

In 1930, the police force changed from a day officer or town marshal and a night watchman, to a four-man paid force, with C. A. Sweeney as chief with a salary of $150 per month. This was the same pay as the two patrolmen, but 25 percent less than the deputy chief got. The pay discrepancy was wiped out in the Depression year of 1933, along with one patrolman's job.

The Antioch Fire Department was organized December 8, 1874, with F. Williams, president; M. S. Levy, secretary; and S. Jessup, foreman. The fire department at this time was entirely volunteer. It came under city control in 1875, but the men received no pay and had to buy their own equipment.

The first paid fireman was in 1925. In 1930, Charles Sweeney joined the department as the second paid man. He later became the first paid fire chief. In 1925, the first purchase of fire equipment was made by the city. This was a mechanized Ford chassis chemical truck that went into

July 4th was always an important day in Antioch since July, 4, 1851, when Antioch was so named. Looking west on Second Street. In the distant left is the Antioch Hotel (The Arata Building). To the right is seen the Arlington Hotel. Photo taken about 1890.

the metal scrap drive of WWII. It was supplemented by a four-wheel hose cart that was towed by the truck or any vehicle the firemen could commandeer to pull it to a fire.

Water has always been a problem for Antioch. At first, they tried dikes, water wheels, windmills and finally, a reservoir to store water for the dry season.

Not much is written of the early water problems, but there were old wells and the brackish water they often supplied, complete with germs. The cisterns gathered water rains, and how wonderful it was when a good well was bored.

In 1869, George A. Dodge, upon a block of the most elevated ground in the place, was engaged in constructing a reservoir, by excavation and embankment, with a view to supplying the town with water. His schemes contemplated a circular embankment averaging 50 feet in breadth at the base and a diameter of 130 feet across the top of the basin. Until this time, water had been distributed by the means of cartage and pumps by wind power. However, the development of a never-failing stream and pipe stream and pipelines conferred a great benefit upon the community.

The first petition to reach the new town board in 1872, from town citizens concerning water, urged the town government to sink an artesian well for public water. There is no record of any action on this petition. In March 1873, J. Miller and Van Phillips got a franchise to supply the inhabitants with water, and that gave Antioch its first step into the water business. In 1875, the town board ordered seven wells bored on as many street corners throughout the town for public use. In the same year, the board reserved all water rights for the town in the area of the wharf to be built along the river between G and H streets; franchise was given to Joseph Galloway.

Late in 1875, W. W. Smith came back to Antioch with his plan for the West Side Irrigation District, which wanted to run a canal from some fresh water lake (name unknown). The city board agreed that Smith could bring this canal into the city at the mouth of Wyatt Slough on what is now J Street. Nothing ever came of this plan.

View of Antioch, northwest from the roof of the school, about 1890. Note the water tower in the upper right on F Street, between 4th and 5th streets. Schooner seen center top; Kimball home and lumber yard buildings can be seen center toward the top - J. T. Belshaw home, left, with the Cooney house and the Bullock homes next. Fifth Street can be seen lower right.

Late in 1876, contractor Wm. H. Dearien erected a 30,000-gallon water tank to supply the engines, mines and the town of Antioch with water. It was Antioch's first water works. The tank was 30 feet above ground, 16 feet high and 20 feet in diameter. It was erected on Kimball (F) Street at the property line between the present Hornback and Marchetti homes. In January 1878, W. W. Belshaw, who had hired contractor Dearien and his company, was granted a franchise to lay waterlines and provide water service for the residents. Prior to this time, water was carted from house-to-house in barrels. In 1903, Antioch finally established a permanent water system. In March of that year, the citizens voted 120 to 8 approval of the community's first bond issue of $22,000 for a waterworks and $8,000 for a sewer system. The city had begun regulating sewer construction in 1876.

Rule No. 1 for the users of the new water system was that there would be no unnecessary waste of water. In 1912, another water problem appeared. This time, it was severe enough to cause the citizens to vote for the bonds of $10,000 to buy and install an electric pumping plant and another $3,000 for buying and installing water meters at the same time they approved an additional $18,000 for a town hall, fire engine house and jail.

The town claim of 3 square miles was cut back to .7 of a square mile during this time by Supreme Court decision, because at no time after the act of 1872, did the town claim jurisdiction over the outside limits of the town specified then.

In 1913, the voters approved a $25,000 water bond issue to pay for a filtration plant, new discharge pipes, electric pumping equipment and replacement of older lines with larger ones.

The Antioch water supply for domestic and other purposes was carried as 'raw' water to the various parts of town in 10-8-6- and 4-inch pipes. The mains were arranged so that in the case of fire, the domestic supply could be turned off and the water carried directly to where it was needed.

Three hundred pounds of pressure could be developed if needed, but generally 110 to 115 pounds of pressure was used. In 1916, a chlorination plant was installed, and the river water now passed through this plant before it went into the main.

Then came the roughest water problem of all. The dependable and endless water supply of the San Joaquin River suddenly disappeared during the summer months, leaving Antioch with brackish, useless saltwater the filtration plant could not handle. The use of Sacramento River water for extensive

A float in another Fourth of July celebration. Far left is the L. Meyers Store. Behind the trees is the Bank of America; next is the Wall Shoe Store and Arlington Hotel.

irrigation of rice plantings in Glenn and Colusa counties so affected the runoff of fresh water into the Delta area during the summer, that the tides were intruding saltwater into the area. The river became so low in Antioch, that it threatened shipping and the water supply. Five-gallon cans were for home use. [Editor's note: presumably fresh water for domestic use.] The result was the suits against the rice growers, which threatened bankruptcy to the "richest farming valley in the world!" This legal action sought to force the rice growers and other users of river water to limit the intake so as to leave enough for Antioch.

The question seemed to divide between saltwater barriers to keep tidewaters back or a storage system to regulate and provide an even flow of mountain water throughout the year. In the Antioch suit of 1919–20, the Antioch Trustees applied to the courts for a temporary injunction, that the users of water be enjoined from taking more water than allowed by the certain flow of the rivers. The lower court granted the injunction, but the rice growers appealed, and the Appellate Court reversed the decision and denied the injunction.

Antioch citizens dug into their pockets and in 1922, approved a $96,000 bond issue to build the reservoir near the present-day golf course. Completed in 1926, it had a capacity of 60 million gallons. In 1928, another bond issue of $35,000 was passed, and it raised the reservoir dams so that it would hold 237 million gallons, covering 50 acres, with a spillway at the elevation of 163 feet above sea level.

After the rice growers' case, the State Water Plan envisioned the Central Valley System. It became a federal project during the Depression of the 1930s. The Contra Costa Canal is a small unit of this large valley plan which is still developing, but it is lending security to Antioch's water supply. The first water flowed in the canal in 1940.

South side of Second Street at G, about 1895. Joslin harness Shop is to the left, while O'Brien Hall is to the right.

Antioch contributed members of its citizens to public service; As State Senators: 1886, J. P. Abbott; 1900, C. M. Belshaw; 1894, C. M. Belshaw; 1924, Robert P. Easley. Board of Supervisors of Contra Costa County: 1854 and 1873 - 1882, J. C. McMaster; 1866, R. B. Hard; 1919, R. J. Trembath. County Sheriff: 1894 - 1934, R. R. Veale. County Tax Collector, 1937, R. R. Veale (was appointed and died in office). County Coroner: 1892, J. C. McMaster. County Surveyor: 1873, Russell Eddy; County Physician, 1897 - 1903. Dr. E. E. Brown; Purchasing Department (formed by order of the Board of Supervisors), Jan.1923 - 1929, J. T. Belshaw.

In 1851, a bill in the California State Legislature passed and officially named the county Contra Costa County. In 1865–66, the county's name was again discussed with some wanting the name changed to Diablo, while others felt the name meaning "devil" was not appropriate. The matter was dropped until 1872, when the residents of the eastern part of Contra Costa County proposed a division of the county. The part east of Port Chicago with sections from San Joaquin, Sacramento and Alameda counties would form a new county called Montezuma. Antioch would be the county seat. The people of Antioch who had spent so much time in court over land claims, felt that Martinez was too far away for the county seat.

Waving his hat is Hon. Joshua Plummer Abbott, owner of the *Antioch Ledger* from 1870 to 1884, after he was state assemblyman. Dr. Worth Scott George is seated, while his brother, Frank George is standing with the 1866 brass frame Winchester. Seated left to right are Mrs. Frank George and Mrs. W. S. George.

Martinez opposed this proposed county division and said that the railroad would make it a two-hour journey. The division was defeated.

The tax rates of 1906 were $1.44 per $100 on an assessed value of $339,761 and had to raise $4,800 for all city operations, including retiring a bond indebtedness. The budget went up to $5,376 in 1907, but the assessed value climbed even more, and the tax rate dropped to $1.32. In 1919, the voters approved a $55,000 bond issue to build the city hall at Third and H streets.

In 1920, a park commission was formed with representatives from Woman's Club, American Legion, Chamber of Commerce, the City Council, and a member appointed by the other four. From this commission evolved the present city park at Tenth and A streets.

An ordinance of 1921 put Antioch in line with national Prohibition. Many saloons went out of business.

In 1928, Antioch acquired its present garbage dump on Somersville Road and paid Eugene Arata $1,000 for 3.55 acres.

In 1933, Antioch grew south of Tenth Street, and the street names there gave way to the city system of numbers and letters. Repeal of Prohibition came this year, too, and with it, a license fee of $20 per year for dispensers of alcoholic beverages.

Santa Fe Depot built about 1902 at First and J streets. Picture taken 1970.

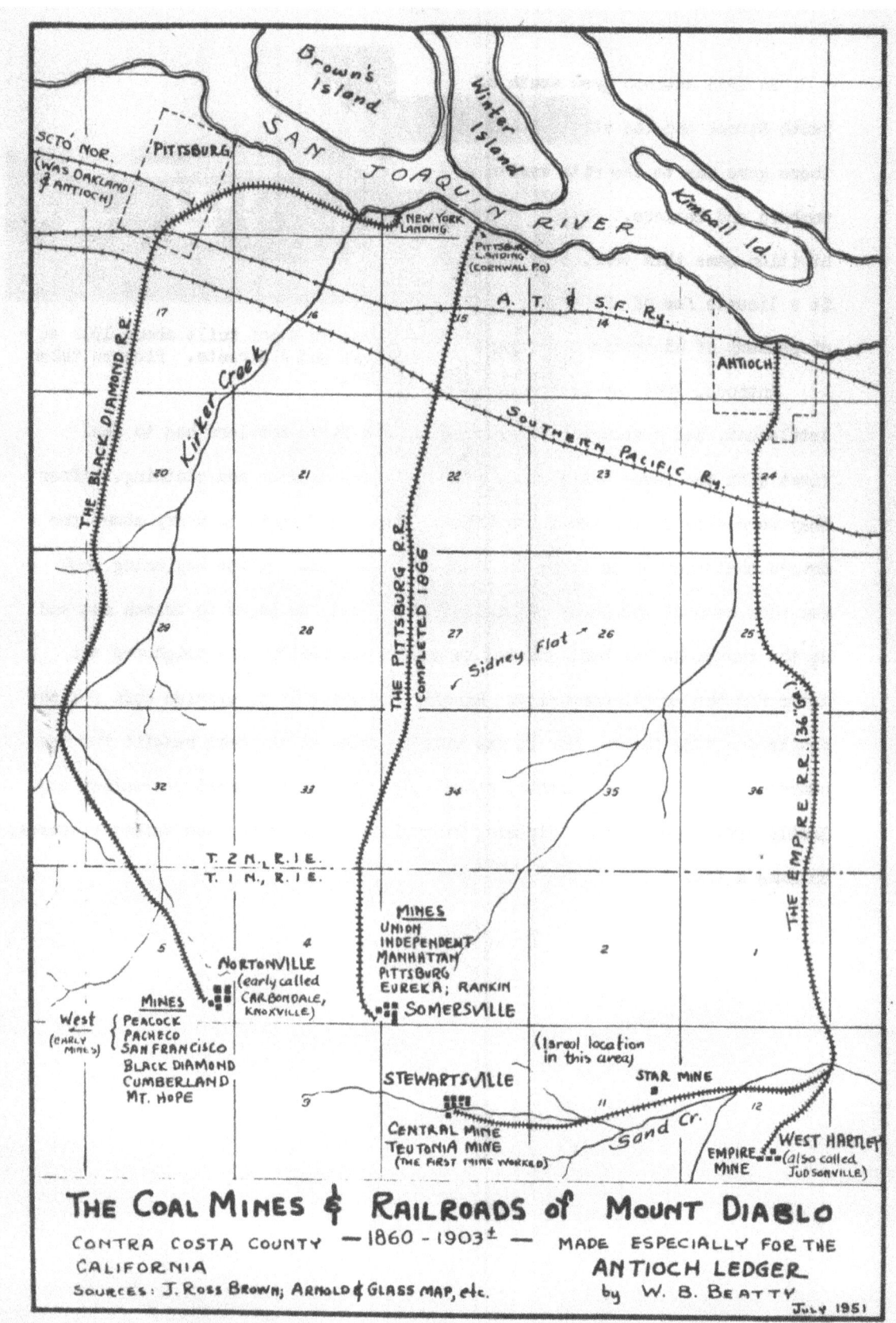

MAP Coal Mines and Trailroads of Mt. Diablo

Chane Stables carry-all had Mr. Boothby as driver between the Arlington Hotel and the Southern Pacific Railroad station at Twentieth and A streets. Pictures taken about 1902. It provided transportation for school children free of charge. Others paid 25 cents.

Union Hall located on Third at H streets. At one time, it was the meeting place for both the Masons and I. O. O. F. Taken 1971.

"The Point" named by W. W. Smith as it is today. The residence is that of the late Jack Rodgers. Taken 1971.

Antioch, like any other new settlement, had a struggle for survival. The first settlers had to deal first with the three basic needs of man: food, shelter and clothing. After they were able to provide those things, they could begin to worry about the things that many of us today feel are so important. In the beginning, each man took care of the needs of his family. Slowly, he began to branch out and do the things he was best adapted to do for his family, his neighbors and later, for the entire community. Finally, he was able to provide work for the people arriving later. Now it was time to think of the best benefit for the community, to provide churches, schools, services, government, recreation, and lastly, city improvements: streets, sidewalks, better water and safety measures, to name a few.

Delta riverfront featuring the Redwood Manufactures Company yard and Johnson and Lanteri Boatyard. Antioch and its waterfront industries located to the east (1910s).

Part II

Industry

As in any new community many industries were started, proved successful for a while, and continued or failed according to the advisability of the industry in the community. Other industries became part of the community in later years. Antioch can trace its growth by the pulse of industry. The first industry in Antioch was the building of brick kilns as early as 1852, by J. C. McMaster, Barker and others. The kilns were located where Mr. Hard's house still stands at the corner of Front and Parsons (First and J) streets. Several of the early homes were built from brick, and most of the homes used these bricks for chimneys. Other remains of kilns have been found at Wyatt and Emmerson (Second and E) streets, another just east of the present-day Fulton Shipyard, while the Holland kilns stood by the river (Jack Little's property). McMaster and Barker leased the W. W. Smith house, when the latter started traveling from place to place throughout the county.

Some of the bricks made were a light-colored clay while most were a red clay. Some sand bricks were made but soon lost out to the more useful and practical red bricks. Locally made bricks were used for the Holy Rosary Church, several homes on Utter (Sixth) Street, Rogers building on Wyatt (Second) Street and the Hollander building at Boobar and Wyatt (G and third) streets. Antioch sent shiploads of brick to San Francisco to help rebuild after the earthquake and fire of 1906.

The development of coal mining about 1860 was the occasion of Antioch's becoming a town in any real sense. Antioch was the shipping point.

Many teams and men were needed to handle the coal. Blacksmiths and mechanics were necessary. Families came and the stores followed. A brick schoolhouse was built and the Stockton boats began to make stops so wharves were built.

Front and side views of the R. B. Hard home, still standing at the corner of J and First streets. Pictures taken 1951.

The first publicized mention of the discovery of coal at Mt. Diablo was made by the *Contra Costa Gazette* of December 11, 1858, which mentioned, "Messer's Rountree, Walker, and Dickson discovered coal November 24, 1858, about halfway from the base of Mount Diablo and Antioch."

George W. Hawxhurst had located coal in 1855. His discovery became the Union Mine. More discoveries were made by Mr. Isreal in 1856, in Horse Haven near Nortonville. In December 1859, Francis Comers, while hunting small game in the hills east of Mt. Diablo, came upon what he supposed was the outcroppings of a vein of coal. The first two veins were broken and unreliable and were abandoned in 1891. The mine discovered by Somers and James T. Cruiksbank was known as the Black Diamond claim and is now surrounded by the ghost town of Nortonville, named after Noah Norton, who built the first house there in 1861. The Central Mine was discovered by W. B. Stewart, T. K. Shattuck and William Hillegas in 1861, and the town was named Stewartsville after the discoverer. Somers associated himself with George W. Hawxhurst, and they prospected in other locations. Somersville was named after Somers who discovered the claim. Somers and Hawxhurst went to the Central Mine to prospect and while there, Norton discovered the Black Diamond claim and built there. It became Nortonville. Hawxhurst and S. B. Whipple, his partner, successfully worked the Union Mine until December 1876. Hawxhurst and J. C. Rouse then bought and opened the Empire Mine. It was soon sold to Mr. E. Judson and Mr. M. W. Belshaw. The town became Judsonville.

At first the coal was hauled upon wagons, from Nortonville to the New York Landing (Pittsburg) or to the Black Diamond Landing (Dow Chemical), and from Somersville to Antioch. Six-horse teams pulling wagons of the "prairie schooner" type were able to deliver 10 tons a day in the dry seasons and 7 to 8 tons during the wet seasons. The wagons were pulled under a "bunker" where they were loaded in 4 or 5 minutes, by gravity.

Lumber Wharf at the foot of E Street. In the foreground are some of the wheels used to haul coal from the mines before 1878.

Somersville in 1878. Named after Francis Somers.

Upon reaching the wharf, the bottom boards of the wagons were removed and the coal was left lying on the dock. The teamsters were paid $1.50 per day, which provided a good living, but no more. Passing steamers stopped to "coal up", schooners and barges carried supplies to scattered users. The barges were used to carry supplies to San Francisco, where the wants of small consumers were delivered by means of carts and wagons. The bulk of the coal supplies used on the Pacific coast came from the Mt. Diablo fields, which furnished 2,000 or more tons per day. With the laying of the railroad from the mines, the Somersville mine moved its shipping point from Antioch to Pittsburg Landing. The only coal coming to Antioch was from the Empire mine of Judsonville and the Central mine of Stewartsville. These mines became productive soon after the other mines began closing down. Much of the first coal was of very poor heat value. One old-timer stated, "A bucket of coal makes two buckets of ash."

An earthquake in 1868 did some damage to the mines and caused part of the porch of the John Marsh home to fall away.

The Empire mine was opened in the fall of 1876, by Hawxhurst and Rouse. Hawxhurst retired, and Judson and Belshaw bought interests in the mine and equipped and built a railroad from Antioch to the mine in 1877. The railroad was 6 miles long. These men soon purchased the Central mine, and in 1881 a branch of the railroad was built to the mine. The incorporation was known as Belshaw and Company. Rouse was resident manager until he retired in August 1884. The official name became Empire Coal Mine and Railroad.

View of Nortonville in the early 1880s.

It is noted that a petition was received by the Antioch Board of Trustees, February 6, 1877, praying the board to create an ordinance granting the right-of-way to Judson and his associates to build a railway through Kimball (F) Street to the waterfront. It was passed. In July 1877, a contractor named Osgood, did the blasting and grading for the railbed and laid ties and the steel. By December 30, 1878, the road was completed from the wharf, on the waterfront at the foot of Kimball Street, to the Empire Mine at Judsonville. The road was inspected by Judson and Belshaw. Wm. H. Dearien, a contractor, had built the bridges over the culverts and the roundhouse. He built a water tank of 30,000-gallon capacity to supply engines, mines and the town with water. There were 10 bridges on the entire system. Three of them were quite large, long and 30-feet high. The remaining seven were of smaller dimensions. One tunnel was 1,000-feet long and very wet at the south end.

August 25, 1877, Engine No. 1, *Empire*, arrived at the coal wharf, at the foot of First and F streets, by schooner. On September 22, S. H. McKellip, locomotive engineer in charge of the rolling stock, fired up the *Empire* and tried her at the waterfront. This was the first engine to turn a wheel in Antioch. On December 22, a large steam water pump and steel waterpipe came to the coal wharf to be installed for the water supply. Captain Boobar of San Francisco, drove the piles for the coal wharf at the foot of Kimball Street. The wharf had a frontage of 250 feet.

Empire Mine located at Judsonville. Miners are unidentified.

Engine No. 2 *Jennie E. Belshaw*, stands by the Empire Railroad roundhouse. S. K. McKellips stands by the throttles, while George Hawxshurt, superintendent of the Empire Mine, stands by the roundhouse. To the west, left to right, are the Bullock, Cooney and J. T. Beslshaw home. The first two still stand on the south side of Fourth Street, between F and G streets.

Engine No. 1 *Empire*. Looking out the cab window is William Bullock, next man to his right is S. H. McKellips, then Louis Dahnken, head brakeman and Nick McVeigh, second brakeman, (right to left) Others unidentified.

Original crew of the Empire Railroad are left to right, Bill Bullock, fireman; Elmer Page, brakeman; S. H. McKellips, engineer; Putnam Reed, brakeman.

The water was so bad in the Empire Mine that Belshaw closed it down in 1881. It had a 31-degree slope down 1,000 feet, to the three veins of coal, "The Little Vein," "The Clarke Vein," and the 4-foot "Black Diamond Vein." Belshaw came back 1 mile from the Empire Mine and put in a railroad "wye" [Editor's note: A wye is a triangular junction joining 3 rail lines.] and ran the road up to Stewartsville, the Central Mine. This road ran 3 miles up the canyon past the old Corcoran place. The Central Mine had been opened in 1870 by running a 1,000-foot tunnel. Belshaw ran a slope of 30 degrees to the coal veins there.

Engine No. 2, the *Jennie E. Belshaw*, arrived in 1883, was larger than No. 1, the *Empire*. *Empire* was a 15-ton Baldwin, while *Jennie* was a 22-ton engine made by Marsclutes and Centrell Company of San Francisco.

The railroad was a 3-foot gauge, link and pin couples and had handbrakes only on all cars. There were no brakes on the engines, and they were stopped with the reverse lever only. There was a grade all the way to the mines. The company never had an accident to train or engine. There were 30 5-ton, bottom-dump coal cars, two 1,500-gallon square tank water cars and one 3,000-gallon tank water car. Fresh water had to be hauled to the mines as the engines at the mines could not use alkali water. There were also two 30-foot flat cars and a 30-foot combination coach for freight and passengers.

Robert Leam was the mine superintendent; J. T. Belshaw, a brother of the mine owner, ran the store in Antioch at Wyatt and Boobar streets. They employed between 150 and 200 miners at a wage between $3 and $4 per day. The railroad crew included one engineer, $120 per month; one fireman, $50 per month; and two brakemen, $50 per month, each. They did all kinds of work besides their regular duties. (No Unions, no Strikes!) From 1884 to 1890, D. O. McKellips was engineer and S.H. McKellips acted as conductor.

Around 1890, Belshaw ran a line to the Hartley Mine, 1 mile above the Empire Mine, up a small valley. Still later, just over the ridge, a mine called the "West Harley," was opened. A spur railroad ran from the Stewartsville branch to this mine, and it was about 1 mile from the main line to the bunkers there. In 1898, all the mines shut down, but June 3, 1899, they were reopened by C. M. Wilson, all except the Empire Mine.

S. H. McKellips was again at the locomotive throttle, and Dave Rouse was the mine superintendent. Wilson later skipped out owing all the employees. When Wilson took over, he had to raise the railroad tracks at the wharf (Kimball Street) to give the Santa Fe Railway the legal overhead clearance. The cars on the Santa Fe siding were loaded by means of a chute from the coal line. On September 20, 1902, Senator Charles Belshaw sold the entire business to a contractor and removal started 3 days later. The tonnage and value of the Contra Costa County Coal operations from 1867–1902, was 2,500,000 tons, valued at $14,500,000.

The discovery of hard coal [Editor's note: Antracite coal] in Oregon and Washington in the 1880s cut down on the value and the demand for the Mt. Diablo soft coal [Editor's note: Bituminous coal] and by 1902 caused the local mines to close for good.

About 1862 or 1863, copper was discovered near Antioch. Antioch was the distinction of having a first copper smelter in California in that year. It was a small reverberatory furnace. Coal was cheap and was obtained from the Mt. Diablo mines to be used as the fuel. A matte [Editor's note: A matte is the phase in which the principle metal being extracted is recovered prior to a final reduction process to produce blister copper.] containing 45 to 48 percent copper was produced. Low-grade oxidized ores were mixed with the sulfides, and the ores were not roasted before smelting. The mines were located in the nearby hills and across the valley in what is now termed the Foothill Copper Belt.

Fifteen to 25 dollars a ton was paid, according to the richness. Hope rose with the smelting works. A chimney 75-feet high accompanied the furnace with promises of 30 to 40 more chimneys to follow, if

Trestle at extreme right at the F Street Coal Wharf. Coal came on the 36-inch narrow-gauge railroad and loaded by chutes to the barges. Coal came from Judsonville, Stewartsville, and West Hartley during the 1880s, furnishing much coal for San Francisco and steamers plying the San Joaquin and Sacramento rivers. The Forman house is seen to the left.

the first was a success in reducing the ore brought from Copperopolis. No more chimneys were built. As was the case with several smelters of this time, Antioch's was short-lived. The chimney stood many years (at A Street, near the Southern Pacific Railroad tracks), a monument to dead hope.

Petroleum was first bored for near Antioch in 1865. Paying quantities were never obtained in those early years.

One of the oldest mercantile firms in Antioch, known today as the Antioch Lumber Company, was founded in 1864, by Galloway and Boobar. Henry F. Beede went to work for this company soon after his arrival in Antioch in 1869. Galloway retired in 1877, and the company became the Rouse, Forman and Beede Lumber Company. During these years, the lumber office was located on the northeast corner of Wyatt and Galloway (Second and H) streets. The later Casino Theater building (Antioch Glass and Mirror Company), Front and Galloway (First and H) streets, was at one time the location of a warehouse of the lumber company. There were grain and hay warehouses extending along the river bank where the Santa Fe warehouse (green pack shed) stood until burning in the summer of 1962. The hay warehouse burned and was rebuilt and later sold. The lumber company purchased the Grange building which is its present location (Wyatt and Emmerson streets) and has been since 1883. The lumber shed was then built at its present site. Around 1880, the company became Rouse, Beede and Abbott and remained as such until Rouse sold his interest to Captain A. H. Simpson, and the present firm, BAS, was incorporated in February 1907, with Simpson as president and Ralph Beede as the first secretary. The name was the Antioch Lumber Company.

Picture of the Rouse, Beede and Abbott Lumber Co. after it moved its office to its present location at First and E streets in 1883. The building had been built by the Antioch Grange in the 1870s.

The Beede, Abbott, and Simpson Lumber Company as incorporated and renamed the Antioch Lumber Company as it appears in 1970.

During the early years, lumber was imported from Oregon and Washington Territory. The sale of this lumber was found in the surrounding districts, large quantities being shipped up the Sacramento and San Joaquin rivers by both boat and sail. Antioch was essentially a distributing point. They carried a stock of from 1.5-million-to 2-million feet of lumber. Under the watchful eye of the senior Beede, the firm did a general lumber and jobbing business, having a well-equipped planing mill in connection with the plant. It was added to the firm about 1904, with the purchase of the distillery building at the southeast corner of Brown and Manhatten (Third and C) streets. The distance of the mill and lumber office from the warehouse used for storing doors and other materials, made necessary the changing of the latter to the present yard in 1911. The mill finished and delivered all kinds of building materials to the trade then and continue to do so today. The corporation was capitalized for $100,000. On the death of H. G. Beede in 1926, then president and manager, Ralph Beede became the active manager. It is thought that the Antioch Lumber Company is the oldest lumber concern in the state still doing business from its original location.

Planing [Editor's note: To create a flat or level surface.] Mill of the Antioch Lumber Company, located at Third Street and extending from B to C streets. Note the cargo ship tied up at the Distillery Wharf on A Street.

View of the waterfront showing the lumber company's planing mill. Just behind it is the one section of the old distillery, still standing. In the center is seen the lumber shed and yard with office across the street and the coal wharf just beyond and to the right. The Santa Fe Railroad trestle is shown center right. This is the view of the river looking towards Pittsburg. The corner of Kimball Island is seen in the upper right. Photo taken about 1910.

The Casino building was built on the site of the lumber warehouse and skating rink. In 1905, Belshaw used it as a store while his new building (Masonic Hall) was being constructed. It was again a warehouse and at last was torn down for the Casino Theater. When the sloped floor for the theater was built, an Indian burial ground was found under the warehouse floor. Ralph Beede had conceived the original idea of the theater and built it in partnership with Ferd Stamm. Beede was very active in local government for years as town clerk and town treasurer.

In 1865, I. Lobree started a pottery establishment as did several others, but the only company to survive for any length of time was the Albion Pottery, started by I. Nicholson in 1868. There was found an unlimited supply of the best quality potter's clay from which the finest porcelain could be made. Both hard and soft clay in various colors with different proportions of kaolinite, silica, feldspar, lime and magnesia were located. Potteries met with sufficient success to prove it could be done if properly managed. Nicholson embarked on this enterprise on the site at Wyatt and Robertson (Second and K) streets. He engaged in the manufacture chiefly of chimney and sewer pipes, terra cotta and stove linings. He employed six to eight men. The buildings were one story in height and covered a space of 100-feet by 150-feet. The company eventually went out of business. Antioch Distillery Company was started by George Russell, William Knight and

This pottery building is thought to be that of I. Lobree. It was located at the site of the Fulton Shipyard of today. It was on the Biglow Ranch.

George Gruenwald in the spring of 1869. It had a capacity of 1,000 gallons. They built in the location of the later planing mill (C between Third and Fourth streets) and built their own private wharf to the river at the foot of A Street.

Antioch Distillery, later the California Distilling Company, located between C and A streets on land. Fourth Street to the north. The only remaining part is the warehouse shown to the extreme left. To the right center is the point where the Jack D. Rodgers house stood. A Street wharf is center left.

In 1870, it was consolidated with the Brannan Street, Pacific and South San Francisco Distilleries and became a stock company. It was continued thus for only 6 months when Mr. Jost was joined in partnership by Aaron Adler, the firm becoming Jost and Adler. After that, many valuable improvements were made including the installation of new machinery and warehouses. The capacity rose to 2,400 gallons per day, in which a revenue of $2,100 per day was paid. They distilled bourbon, rye and other spirits and also produced German compressed yeast. Two thousand pounds per week were turned out and shipped to the San Francsico markets. They employed about 20 men.

The Antioch Distillery became the California Distilling Company in 1882, when Alder Yoast, supervisor, started making whiskey, fruit brandy and dry and sweet wines.

The abundance of tule around Antioch brought into being two industries both comparatively short-lived. San Francisco provided a large market for such articles.

Antioch waterfront view of after 1900, shows the remains of the Jost Distillery. In the background is the lumber shed and yard, office and coal wharf. Santa Fe train is approaching the trestle.

The Joe Ross store located at the corner of G and Third streets.

The Hartley two-story building is located on the west side of G Street between Second and Third streets. Note the two chimneys on the south wall. Taken 1971.

Antioch railroad station

Carman and Israel Grocery of the 1870s. First and I streets, the present Jack Wolfe Hardware Store.

So, in 1975, a company was organized for the purpose of preparing tule for the manufacturing of mattresses and such like articles of upholstery. In 1878, Mr. Cooley embarked in and later perfected the venture of making tule covers for bottles for the San Francisco market.

Pioneer Soda Works was among the first establishments of its kind in the country. It was founded by John Gagen, who ran it until it passed into the hands of John Reilly in 1881. They manufactured all manner of aerated waters including soda, ginger ale, sarsaparilla, and cider.

Site of the Donlon Drayage building of the 1870s, later the site of the Antioch Ice and Fuel Co. Located on the southwest corner of G and Third streets.

Chase, Main Street Livery Stable manager. Located at the northwest corner of I and Third streets.

The Harley building is seen on the far right.

(Editions of) the Antioch *Ledger* of the 1870s carried the following advertisements:

    Carman and Isreal, Main Street - Groceries, Cash prices

    R. Eddy - Civil Engineer, Survey and Real Estate Agent

    Union Hotel and City Bakery, Jos. Ott - Prop.

    Madame LeQuenel, Galloway and Brown streets, Milliner and Dressmaker

    S. Jessup - Carpenter and Builder, Main and Marsh streets

Wolf, Kahn and Co. - Wholesale and Retail dealers in general merchandise. Wheat, barley bought at San Francisco market prices. Agriculture and harvesting machines.

Chase and Robbins Livery Stables

Gunsmith - S. G. Page, Galloway Street

J. D. McCarty - Blacksmith, Main and Wyatt

City Market - Main Street, Hard's Building, J. C. McMaster and Co. Prop.

Antioch Hotel - Wyatt and Main, Randall - Prop. Temperance, Meals 37½ cents, Beds 37½ cents

"Il Figaro" V. Remfree - Barber opposite National Hall

DeWitt's Drug Store.

Donlon Drayage business was started around 1870 by the elder Peter Donlon. The Donlons built a home and later a large two-story frame building on a concrete foundation, which originally housed the Joe Ross grocery, at the corner of Boobar and Brown (G and Third) streets. The home was moved to Brown (Third) Street where it stands today, just east of the Antioch Ice and Fuel Company. The two buildings of the Ice and Fuel Co. originally were the first city-owned town hall. The fire equipment was kept in the back section of the building and the jail was the building that stores the ice today. The Donlan's bought these buildings when the present City Hall was completed in 1919. The sons, James and Peter A. Donlon, owned and operated this business for many years. James Donlon later became a member of the city Board of Trustees as the result of the water problem, later becoming the last president of the board and the first mayor of the City of Antioch, a city of the sixth class when its city government was reorganized with a city council and mayor.

View of upper D Street wharf on the river with Thomas Gain's home on the left..

The Board of Trustees received a petition November 9, 1889, from M.D. Keeney to erect a paper mill. It was passed. Keeney came from Wilmington, Illinois. He had been a success in paper milling in spite of the misfortune of having three of his mills destroyed by fire and the fourth destroyed by flood. He recognized the natural advantages, resources and facilities of Antioch over other places in the state. In November, he purchased six blocks, with a 50-foot roadway to deep water, in the western part of town and began to build. The main building in which the machinery was located, was 40 by 140 feet, to which was attached a bleaching room 30 by 40-feet and an engine room of the same size. The latest and most-approved machinery was placed in position, and the whole plant by May cost about $30,000. The plant went into operation in May 1890 and produced from 4 to 5 tons of straw paper per day. The mills were running on 30-pound paper and turning out a superior article in spite of the fact all the chaff was mixed with the straw. About 2 tons of straw were used to make 1 ton of paper. The paper was worth about $60 per ton at wholesale. At the start, the mill employed 15 men but soon increased to 25. The present site covers the blocks from the Santa Fe tracks to Marsh (Fourth) and O'Brien to West (L to O) streets. At various times during the first years the board received petitions asking to close off another street or streets as the plant expanded to its present boundaries. When first established, it was known as the Antioch Paper Mill. An interesting ad appeared in the June 28, 1890, *Ledger*:

> Keeney and Sons - Straw wanted for the paper mill. We trust farmers will endeavor to have straw separated from the chaff at the threshing machine. Cannot make use of headed straw unless chaff is separated from it. Pay better price for stubble portion if free from weeds.

Another newspaper article of May 5, 1906, states:

> The steamer *San José* arrived this week with a cargo of cottonwood, consigned to the California Paper and Board Mills. The manufacture of paper from pulp, using the raw material, is a new departure for the mill in Antioch. Heretofore, the pulp was secured from New York at a cost of $400 freight per car. Careful investigation has proved that there is enough cottonwood in California to fill the demand here and that the texture of the fibre is as good as the Eastern wood. The local plant at once started to build an additional mill to handle this product and install a 400-horsepower dynamo to run the necessary machinery.

H. D. Keeney, the senior member of the local firm, patented an invention valuable to paper manufacturers. He and his son, Will, went to Holyolke, Massachusetts, in June 1897, to introduce it. Emerson and Collins Kenney continued operations here.

In 1900, Peter and James Brown bought the mill, added new machinery and increased the output. In March 1912, the plant became the property of the Paraffine Paint Company of San Francisco and was incorporated as the California Paper and Board Mill. Improvements and changes were made including healthier and drier surroundings in which the employees worked, the main raw material entering into the operations is obtained locally and stored in huge pyramids in a field west of town, later the Riverview High School area.

The *Hespian*, a frequent visitor, tied up to one of Antioch's wharfs.

Antioch's first telephone exchange was founded in January 1882; in 1893, 33 subscribers; in 1905, 56; and in 1926, there were 341 telephones.

The post office in Antioch of the 1880s to 1920s was a political football moving from location to location depending on whether the Democrats or Republicans were in office. Two of the locations were the rear of the Baker Hardware store, with a Boobar (G) Street entrance (Famous Fashion store) and the L. Meyers Dry Goods Store at Wyatt and Galloway (Second and H) streets.

A point of interest was the boat travel or the 1880s as later compared to the train. April 3, 1886, it was noted that fare from San Francisco to Stockton was 10 cents compared to the train from Port Costa to Stockton at 2:30 p.m. The fare by boat in December 1887 from San Francisco, was 75 cents. In 1890, the boats made regular calls at Martinez, Port Costa, Antioch, and Black Diamond to load freight and passengers. Tom Uren, who was brought to Antioch as a baby in 1877, relating an experience of the late 1880s:

> I can remember as a young boy, I wheedled a dollar from my mother. I took the boat to San Francisco. That cost 10 cents. I'd buy coffee and three doughnuts for 5 cents when I got to the City. I could take in the Orpheum and sit in '******-heaven'[Editor's note: censored] for 10 cents more. Most of the time I would have money left over to have a six-course dinner on the boat coming back that night.

Uren spoke about the fisherman bringing their salmon catch into the Antioch wharf every afternoon, and the wharfinger [Editor's note: A "wharfinger" is the individual who takes custody of and is responsible for goods delivered to the wharf] would chute them into the warehouse at the foot of Boobar (G) Street and box them. The boat from Sacramento to San Francisco would pick up 200 or 300 fish every day for them. Others relate that the fish taken from the river would feed them when little else was to be had. They caught salmon, catfish, striped bass and giant sturgeon that had to be hauled from the river by block and tackle, to be shipped to San Francisco to sell their caviar to the Nob Hill residents.

An early business of Antioch was the Baker and George Drug Store in the O'Brien Building first floor. Located on Second Street next to the Joslin home and harness shop.

The coming of the railroads first to San Pablo and Tulare, then the Southern Pacific in 1878, and later the San Francisco and San Joaquin Valley Railroad (Santa Fe) in 1900, seemed to increase the possibility of Antioch being the hub of river commerce. H. F. Beede had gotten the right of way for the railroad line in 1899. Neither railroad offered convenient connections elsewhere, and in fact, for many years the Santa Fe had its eastern terminus in Antioch.

We seemed to be the ideal spot for shipping freight and passengers from the Delta area north at Rio Vista and east to Stockton.

The river could not meet the challenge of the railroad improvements and the highway development. The river thus became something more to enjoy and use as each person saw fit.

The Jarvis brothers built a shipyard in the early years which is still operating under the ownership of the Fultons. The early yard built boats and small ships and had a slip-way on which repairs could be made on ships, passenger ferries and the like.

Some of the business ads appearing in (editions of) the *Ledger* of the 1890s included:

Brown and George Farm machinery - hardware, cutlery, stoves, furniture, matting, wallpaper, Bedrock prices

Otto E. Klengel - south side Wyatt, halfway between Boobar and Galloway, "Antioch's leading harness maker"

Eureka Market - Noakes and Hough, Best fresh beef, mutton and pork

D. McCartney - dealer in fruit, groceries, confectionary, Wyatt Street; Agent for Liverpool, London

River Express Co., Est. 1878, Stockton, San Francisco, Oakland and Berkeley - Daily, Antioch agent - F. Dahnken

H. B. Reed, Undertaker, Marsh and Kimball streets

Joe Ross - Groceries, Coffee a Specialty, Brown and Boobar streets

Ludinghouse and Son, Blacksmith and Carriage Maker

M. H. Jacobs - General Dry Goods and Grocery, hardware, paints and oils, Main and Front streets

Stamm Brothers - Boots and Shoes, Wyatt Street

Nelson Peterson - Antioch 1867 Blacksmith, Drown and Galloway streets, investor of Peterson's cultivator, Deals in machinery, wagons and buggies

Jarvis Brothers Shipyard, the site of the present Fulton Shipyard. On the slip for repairs is the ferry, *Express*. Capacity is 250.

Otto E. Klengel, Antioch's leading harness maker is seen in front of his shop around 1890; located on the south side of Second Street, half way between G and H streets.

Brown and Baker Hardware Store located, in the 1890s on the northeast corner of Sedon and G streets. Later, it became the Antioch Hardware and Furniture Company, then Trembath and Frederickson, and lastly the House Hardware. Today it is the Famous Fashion store. Pictured from left to right are Uncle Billy Forman, Ina Baker, George Hawxhurst, Jean Baker Turner, J. Rio Baker, Ben Turner and Frank Biglow.

Nelson Peterson Blacksmith and factory for Peterson's cultivator. Located at the northeast corner of Third and H streets. Picture of the shop in 1937.

Dickson, later Arlington Hotel as it appeared in 1932 on the north side of Second Street between G and H streets. This is a parking lot today.

Antioch Drug Store - Drs. DeWitt and Rattan, Full line of stationary, school books, pure drugs, chemicals, patent medicines, perfumery, fancy goods, toilet Articles

Morrisey's Corner - Northwest Wyatt and Galloway streets

Palace Hotel - Northeast corner Wyatt and Boobar streets

Kelley Funeral Home - Main Street

Timms Millinery - Wyatt Street between Galloway and Main

Biglow and Joslin City Draymen - Antioch leave orders at Post Office

Antioch Lumber Company- Rouse, Beede and Abbott

Dickinson Hotel (renamed Arlington) New Building - 40 rooms special rates to families centrally located

Brown and Baker Hardware Wyatt and Boobar streets (Later became Antioch Hardware and Furniture Co. J. C. Rouse - Prop. then became Trembath and Frederickson Hardware).

Bank of Antioch building built in 1923 on the northeast corner of Second and H streets. The bank later merged with Bank of America. Picture taken in 1970.

The Bank of Antioch was established September 12, 1891. The capital stock was $100,000. Officers were S. G. Little, president; J. Rio Baker, vice-president; H. F. Harkinson, secretary/treasurer. H.H Beede and J. C. Rouse and the above, comprised the Board of Directors.

View of northeast Antioch from the water tower. To the left, are the railroad cars and tracks of coal railroad. Luddinghouse Blacksmith and Carriage Makers. Center is Joe Cervans Machine Shop. Lower center is the G. W. Kimball home, with a mulberry tree to the east of the house. The lumber office and shed are shown center right.

The First National Bank Building built in 1912 on Second and G streets.

The bank building was constructed in 1923, at the cost of $23,000 at Second and H streets. It was taken over by the Bank of America of California in 1930 and merged with them in December 1934. It became the National Trust and Savings Bank.

The First National Bank of Antioch was organized in October 1910. The capital stock was $25,000. Antioch Bank of Savings was organized at the same time. The Capital stock was $50,000. Business began January, 3, 1911. The officers were the same for both banks: J. L. Harding, president; J. A. West, vice president and manager; Herbert A. West, cashier.

The directors were E. C. Worrell, J. Arata, M. Beata, W. C. Williamson, J. C. Prewett plus the president and vice president. The bank building was at the southwest corner of Second and G streets.

The sand dunes between Antioch and Marsh Landing (PG&E Steam Plant) were used by different companies engaged in construction of roads and other projects. Contra Costa County was second in California in the amount of sand, gravel and crushed stone produced. The Antioch area is a great contributor.

Do you remember in 1902 when:

The Antioch wharves, two oil tank lines and two steamboat lines, landed boats every day at Antioch to and from San Francisco? Fare 50 cents? Freight 25 cents per ton?

Jim "Clock" Hoien, only watchmaker shop in town? Expert watchmaker and did photography?

Herman G. Newbert, night clerk at the Arlington Hotel?

Turner Brothers, best barbers in the country? Shaving Parlor in the Arlington Hotel?

L. Meyer and Company, largest and best-equipped merchandise store operated by the Meyers brothers at the northwest corner of Second and H streets?

El Campanile Theatre was built in 1928, Second and G streets. The school bell hangs in the center arch. Picture taken in 1937.

The J. R. Baker Hardware store? J. Rio Baker was Antioch postmaster, school trustee, director of the Antioch Bank, president of the city trustees and county treasurer from 1912 until his death in 1922.

A. J. Markowitz, a merchant tailor who preferred custom tailoring to rebuilt tailoring?

Dr. W. S. George, physician and surgeon? He was health officer, member of the city trustees, a school trustee, and surgeon for the Southern Pacific and Santa Fe railroads.

Hose Cart Race July 4, 1910. Pictured left to right, Manuel Azevedo, Turner, (?), Charles Sweeney, Arch Waldie, Firby, Brown, Al Cooney, Brown (?), (?), Fred Wolcott, Ferd Stamm, Willie Griffin, Nick Petrovich.

West side of G Street between Second and Third streets as it appeared in 1937, north of Joe Ross Store.

Frank M. Wills, real estate and insurance business for Antioch? C. T. Barnett, the Santa Fe agent? T. P. Shine, dealer in wine and liquor, who owned the "Reception" a popular resort? He later became town marshal.

Ferd Stamm was chief of the volunteer fire department for many years with Peter A. Donlon, senior assistant chief, who later became chief. They put on hose cart races and other contests staged by the firemen at public celebrations.

For Commerce - Boats tied to the lumber pier at the foot of D to E streets. Note the distillery wharf in the background, the Point is seen in the upper center left of the photo.

Beede and Stamm were partners in the first photo-play theater in Antioch (Casino). They built the El Campanil Theatre in 1928, at Second and G streets. Beede later sold his partnership to Stamm, who became sole owner of the theaters of Antioch.

The Hunter Livery, located at the northwest corner of G and Fourth streets, during the turn of the century.

Draying to the 1890s was by horse (No. 11) and wagon. Wharfinger Fred Dahnken had his office at the Antioch Wharf located at the foot of H Street. The gentleman pictured center with his hands in his pockets, is J. P. Abbott. Extreme right is J. Rio Baker, and to his right is Thomas Gaines.

The Lauritzen Transportation Company based its operations at the municipal wharf (J Street) and carried on a successful passenger travel, until railroads and highways changed the interest to speed and wheels. F. C. Lauritzen and brother Chris Lauritzen founded and operated the company, which provided passenger, mail and small freight boat service throughout the Delta area triangle with its corners at Antioch, Sacramento and Stockton. Some of their boats were 100-feet-long and included the *Empress, Duchess, Ellen, Princell, Gwendolyn* and *Doris*. The river in those days supported hundreds of flat-bottomed sailing barges, sailing ships, river steamers and other craft. Chris Lauritzen was active in the operation of the Jersey-Bradford-Webb ferry that preceded the Antioch bridge at the same location.

In February 1919, The U.S. Government appropriated $64,500 for the widening and deepening of Suisun Bay and the San Joaquin River from Antioch to Martinez.

C. Lauritzen commented, "An automobile trip to Sacramento in 1920 was only for the brave and rugged. Three ferries had to be used between Antioch and Rio Vista and the island roads were impossible."

The Antioch-Sherman Island toll bridge was the golden link of the Victory Highway, the direct ocean road.

The movement for this bridge was started by Roy V. Davis, president of the Antioch Chamber of Commerce in 1921, with the bridge committee, organized in 1922. The final developed after the Delta Bridge Corporation was organized in 1923, after the investigation of Avery Hanford and Oscar H. Klatt, president and vice-president of the American Toll Bridge Company of San Francisco. They secured approval of

Photo of Antioch Bridge taken from the south shore. It shows the center span raised as it was stuck from September 1970 to January 1971.

the Contra Costa Board of Supervisors, the California state engineer and finally the U.S. War Department in December 1923. Construction was begun May 1924, and was opened for use in January 1926.

The piers rose 186 feet above the water and 106 feet above the roadway of the bridge. The total length of the trestle bridge with one fixed steel span is 4,639 feet. The roadway width between curbs is 21 feet. Under the two main spans, clearance is 70 feet, while the lifespan has a clearance of 135 feet. The lift span weighs 600 tons and is elevated by electric motors and counter-balanced slabs of concrete. The counter balances are 106 feet above the driveway and 186 feet above high water. The two main spans allow 270 feet open space with the river 40 feet deep at that point. This allows the largest vessels afloat to pass.

On the Contra Costa shore, the first 869 feet are concrete trestle on a 5 percent grade. The next 912 feet are of steel, on concrete foundations with concrete floor at a 3.1 percent grade, at this point the clearance is 60 feet. From here to the lift span is 1,939 feet with a rise of 10 feet in the distance. Then there are the two 300-foot spans, giving openings of 270 feet each, for the vessels.

From the long spans to Sherman Island are 215 feet where a turn of a right angle is made on a 200-foot radius and the bridge built from here on to the Sherman Island end, 850 feet more is on a grade of 6 percent. The right-angle turn was reconstructed to a straight approach with a gradual sweep at the base, in the late 1950s.

Two small stores west of El Campanile, west to Arlington Hotel and north side of Second Street between G and H.

This view from the water tower, about 1900, shows in the center the Nason-Keeney home. Hunter Livery Stable across G Street. Top left is the paper mill. Top right is the Arlington Hotel and immediately in front and below, is the Ross Grocery Store.

The Casino Theater building. Upper photo: southeast view showing the brick wall and fire escape. Lower photo: southwest view showing the main entrance on H Street at First. Picture taken 1971.

The Schott home on Third Street showing the condition of the streets before paving in 1914 and 1916. Taken about 1905.

The Antioch Bridge was built, owned and operated by the American Toll Bridge Company with contracts let for the complete structure. It cost $2,000,000 and was later sold to the state by the bridge company.

Some interesting facts about Antioch in 1925 are:

Main Elevation, 30 feet; Assessed Valuation, $1,498,197; Tax Rate, $171; Homes, 500; Population, 2,800; Banks, two; deposits, $1,634,158; Paved streets, 111 Blocks; Street Lamps, 100; Electroliers, 64; Manufacturing Establishments, two; Parks, one; Public Schools, two; School Students, 850; Sanitary Sewers, 150 Blocks; Apartment Houses, 10; Churches, four; Fire Houses, one; Fire Engines, two; Fire Hydrants, 52; Fire Alarm System, $3,000, Gamewell; Value Water Works, $190,000 and New City Hall, $65,000.

The Caroline, one of the oldest ferries plying the river between Stockton and San Francisco. This was an excursion of the employees of the Bowers Rubber Works. Taken in the summer of 1908.

Antioch's Band pictured here in 1882, provided music for special events. The drummer died at 23.

Auto Fourth of July Parade about 1912 at Second Street looking west from G Street. The streets were paved in 1914.

Brick School House. Stood on G Street between Fifth and Sixth streets. It was torn down in 1890. One of the two frame buildings are shown to the right.

Mrs. A. B. Schott's home after her husband's death in 1880 until about 1902, which was located on the northwest corner of Tenth and F streets. Then it became the L. Meyers home.

The Mrs. A. B. Schott home built by her son, George, on Third Street just east of the Kimball house. Mrs. Schott lived there until her death in 1917. Note the Congregational Church spire in the background.

Antioch Grammar School, Maggie Williams, teacher.

Part III

Educational, Spiritual and Social Life

As has already been stated, the education of children was always of prime importance to the people of Antioch. Adelia B. Kimball was the first permanent teacher, taking her place as teacher of a half dozen children in the fall of 1850, when she was but 12-years-old.

Adelia Kimball went to Rincon Point School No. 1 in San Francisco in 1855. She took part in several of the school's programs and for one, wrote and took part in an original dialogue entitled, "Fashion." She graduated from the San Francisco High School in January 1863. Her class consisted of four girls and five boys. She married John Schott on September 28, 1863. They lived in Antioch and on Kimball Island, except 22 months spent in Sonoma County. After his death in 1880, Mrs. A. B. Schott lived in Antioch until her death in 1917. After 1880, her home was on the northwest corner of Kimball and Rattan (F and Tenth) streets. Hs son, George, built a home on Third Street, just east of the Kimball home, were he lived from 1905 to 1917.

Antioch Grammar School, Maggie Williams, teacher.

Frame School Building at the same site as the old brick school house. The school stood until 1926.

After the ship's galley, which served as the first school, the next schoolhouse was a small one-room house near Emmerson (E) Street. Following Kimball as teacher was James Cruickshank, who taught a few terms when an exceptionally fine teacher was hired, Mrs. Woodruff. After that, there is record of J. P. Abbott, Warren Abbott and Miss Carpenter as principals.

Little else is known of the Antioch schools until 1865–66, when the census count gave 86 children in Antioch, 71 in school. H. R. Avery was county superintendent with offices at Pacheco. According to his report the Antioch school was maintained for 4 months that year as it operated as a public school for 9 months. Other information for this first year was $421.37 paid in teachers' salaries (this included the board), $449.27 total expenditures, $200 total value of school property. In 1869–70, the county superintendent A. Thurber, reported, "The people of Antioch have erected a fine brick schoolhouse 32 by 50 feet of two stories." The funds were mostly furnished by subscription. The value of school property for that year was given as $4,000.

Nortonville School 1. Will Abrams, 2. Alice Sorgenfrey, teacher in 1900; 3. Alice Lougbev, 4. Sarah Banchero, 5. Louis Ginnocchio, 6. John Buffo, 7. Edna Scauton, 8. Joe Buffo?, 9. Pearl Davis, 10. Bennie Edward, 11. Amelia Ginnocchio, 12. Lorenzo Buffo.

It was noted in February 1883, that school had begun with Mr. Haven as principal. In 1884, the teachers were listed as Miss Williams, Miss Stinchfield and Miss Dixon taking Miss Mitchell's place. Antioch was well known in the eastern part of the county for its fine grammar school and the high standard of its work.

In June 1883, Miss Annie Stinchfield opened a private school for children of the primary grade.

In 1890, the old brick school to which had been added several wooden structures was replaced by a new $15,000, two-story, frame building, 99 by 89 feet, and the former was torn down. They were both at the location of the present John Muir School, (G to H and Fifth to Sixth streets). The small wooden structure to the north housed the primary grades, while the one to south housed the third and fourth grades.

There was one problem with the new school - a bell. It was felt that every school should have a bell with deep, mellow tones. There were no funds with which to purchase one. The trustees ordered one. It arrived May 17, from West Troy, New York. It weighed 1,300 pounds and cost $240. When the school was torn down in 1926, to make way for the John Muir School, the bell was placed in the center arch of the new El Campanil Theatre, where it can be seen today.

As early as 1883–84, there were five students doing high school work as post-graduate courses of the grammar school program in Antioch.

In 1888, the state legislature passed a law providing for a two-year high school course in the public schools. In 1891, after many vain attempts to establish more high schools in California, Superintendent P. M. Fisher of Alameda County, drafted a bill, passed by the Legislature, which established and supported union high school districts, made up of adjoining elementary districts. The course of study was to be arranged by the school board and to prepare students for the state university. A special district tax was to be levied each year for the support of the high schools. This law increased the high schools from 24 in 1890 to 87 in 1894 and was said to be one of the most influential laws in the history of high school education in California.

With the passage of this law, leading citizens of Antioch started a movement to establish a union high school in eastern Contra Costa County, located in Antioch.

They estimated that the support makeup of 12 elementary districts, with a property valuation of $3 million, would be about $1,200 per year. The greatest expense would be the salary of the principal, about $125 per month. The tax rate would be less than $1 million. They felt Antioch was the best location, for it had the largest population in 1890, with 1,030. Antioch could afford adequate room in the best grammar school in the county without further expenditure for a building. Antioch Grammar School graduated more each year than any other district in this part of the county. As a result of a mass meeting held June 20, 1891, A. C. Hartley, T. J. Belshaw and C. F. Montgomery took petitions, to be signed by the trustees of the elementary school districts in eastern Contra Costa County, asking for an election to decide whether or not to join Antioch in forming a union high district. Sixteen districts signed [Editor's note: the petition]. Brentwood did not sign, for it felt it was more centrally located in relation to the districts included.

Martinez and its adjoining districts voted to form a union high school district in July 1891. The central districts of the county formed a union high district.

At the same time, the post-graduate courses which had been maintained in the elementary schools of the county were abolished, and the high school need was imperative.

The election was held July 18, 1891 with 12 of the 16 districts voting in favor of the eastern union high district. The attorney general said, "That since the four districts voting against the formation of the union high district had signed the petition for the election, they were a legal part of the district."

This met with bitter opposition in the districts. The districts included were Live Oak, Iron House, Eden Plain, Lone Tree, Judsonville, Deer Valley, Liberty, Hot Springs, Byron, Black Diamond, Nortonville, Somerville, Stewartsville, Bay Point, Excelsior and Antioch. The Board of Trustees consisted of the presidents of the 16 elementary districts. Antioch was the chosen location and housed the new high school in the second floor of the new Antioch Grammar School. Professor Granville P. Foster, late vice-principal of the Stockton High School, was chosen principal at a salary of $150 per month. A special district tax raised $2,700 to fund costs.

Antioch Union High School opened September 21, 1891, with 16 pupils present, soon increased to 19. There were three grades, Junior, Middle and Senior years. The elementary schools at that time consisted of nine grades. All the pupils registered as Juniors for the first year, which ended June 17, 1892. They remained at work until 6 p.m. almost daily, having arrived at school at 8:30 a.m. The University examiner had visited the school in May and found it satisfactory. The balance in the school fund as of July 1892, was $1,823.65. There was trouble from Byron and Brentwood over the tax levy and the anti-high school agitation.

The trustees decided July 30, 1892, that the regular course prescribed by the state would be taught. That was the course in accordance with curriculum prescribed by the university and would prepare pupils for college. Another class to be included was to prepare young ladies to become teachers in the shortest possible time. Also to be included was a commercial or business course which would prepare the pupils for the active duties of life.

The second year began in August 1892, with 22 students enrolled in the following classes: Middle class, eight students and selective studies, two students. There were 15 classes and only one teacher. Eight classes were taught each day and classes alternated, with Latin taught at recess and bookkeeping at 8:30 a.m. A band was organized. Those against high school continued to find things wrong and discouraged participation in the program.

1893 High School Classes. The five graduates of June 1893, were: Miss Emma Hobson, row one, far right; Franklin T. Schott, row two, first left; Carlton Biglow, row three, fourth from left; Arba Joslin, row three, fifth from left; Frank Wills, row four, far right. Their teacher was Granville P. Foster.

Carlton Biglow as he appeared in his Stanford football uniform, about 1898.

The third year began August 8, 1893, with all three classes represented for the first time. If all of the plans of the trustees had been carried out, there would have been 30 classes. The tax rate of 6 cents allowed only one teacher, so the commercial and teacher training classes had to be curtailed. The term closed with the first graduation on June 16, 1894. Those graduating were Emma Hobson, Carlton Biglow, Arba Joslin, Frankin T. Schott and Frank Wills. All four men went to Stanford and graduated, one in May 1898, and the other three in May 1899.

It was rumored that the school would be closed for an indefinite period, because of the McCabe vs. Carpenter case over tax collection; the State Supreme Court decided in favor of McCabe, the citizen. The attorney general indicated that only section 4 was unconstitutional. A law of 1893 corrected the faults of the original 1891 law and indicated new means of school support.

The fourth year did not begin until April 1895, with Mrs. Margaret Elmore, salary of $100 per month, as teacher. School was in session 2 months with the average daily attendance of 15. In May, County Superintendent Phalin announced that the Antioch High School District had lapsed "on account of not being used, the allotted length of time for school purposes. "The law read A.D.A. [Editor's note: "A.D.A. is an abbreviation of "Average Daily Attendance" which is key to California State funding.] of 10 after the first year for a school term of 9 or 10 months. Antioch argued that this law applied only to districts with an insufficient number of pupils and not to other reasons, and also that during time in session in the 1894–95 school year they had used only the funds provided by the high school district itself. The Union High School was supported at that time by a special district tax.

The State Superintendent of Instruction, after studying all the facts, decided the district had not lapsed. In the fall of 1895, when the trustees applied for $1,700 to defray expenses, the supervisors took it under advisement and as the attorney general stated the district had lapsed, the request for appropriations was refused, and the school was forced to close. In January 1896, the furniture and fixtures were auctioned off. From June 1895 to 1903, there was no high school in Antioch, though some high school work continued in supplementary classes in the grammar school.

Mr. Foster taught until December 1893, when he took over the editorship of the *Ledger* and employed Orville Gridley to teach halftime. Foster paid his salary, taught morning classes and did the administrative work. Foster resigned March 1894, and Mr. Eugene Joralomon of Palo Alto was chosen principal, and his wife was elected his assistant. His salary was $150 per month.

With the passing of new legislation in 1901, the state financial aid for the support of union high schools, we find Alhambra, Diablo, John Swett and Liberty Union high schools being established. There was a general lag of interest in Antioch until H. F. Beede and W. S. Moore, the principal of the Antioch Grammar School, with the help of the newly organized Antioch Woman's Club brought about the union of Antioch, Black Diamond, Somerville and Carbondale districts to form the Riverview Union High School. The Live Oak district was soon separated from the Liberty Union and joined the Riverview Union.

Henry F. Beede was a businessman and civic leader. The high school system was made permanent by his foresight and work.

Riverview Union High School. [Editor's note: Present-day location of the Antioch Historical Museum]

Class picture at Riverview High School.

The school was located at Antioch in the Grammar School building. The assessed value of the district was $1,050,000. The Riverview District was established June 1, 1903, with a sweeping victory. The trustees, elected one from each district, were Antioch, H. F. Beede, president; Somersville, William Laird; Nortonville, John Jones; Black Diamond, W. C. Lewis. W. C. Moore was elected principal of the

Photo of the Class of 1903. Front from left to right, Nellie Beede Kelley, Edna Peters Irvine, Helen Stokes Higgins, May Cooney Smith, Loretta Kelley, Arvilla McMullen Downing, Helen Trythall and Miss Emily Hagmire, teacher. Second row, from left to right, Adelbert Dunton, Francis Cooney, Charles Dickinson, Charles Bassett, Judson Biglow, Bedson Juett, Roscoe Wall, Cyril Viera, Roy Smith. Back from left to right, Jennie Bullock Woolan, Edna Schultz Ward, Miss Glenn, Cassie Redding, Margaret Irwin, Willie Williamson Lynch, Imogene Belshaw Showers, Araminta Evans Olsen, Professor Walter Moore.

Riverview Union High School at $100 per month and $35 from the Grammar School District. Miss Emelie Hagmeyer was the only teacher for the first 2 years. The school opened August 24, 1903, with 32 pupils. In 1906, a science laboratory was constructed in the basement, but instruction was handicapped by the lack of running water and proper sewage despite good apparatus. The commercial work was started that year, too. The year before, another teacher had been added to the staff, Miss Ada Shreve, and Miss Ruth Millard replaced Hagmeyer, who resigned.

The school year 1906–09, there were four grades, 9 through 12, with three teachers, the principal and 68 registered pupils. Eleven pupils returned from Black Diamond, Somersville and Nortonville after the mines closed. They came by launch which landed at the Lauritzen wharf near the Santa Fe Station. These pupils were responsible for their transportation to and from Black Diamond.

The first class to graduate from Riverview Union High School was in May 1907. It was a class of seven, six of whom were part of the original 32 who enrolled in 1903. They were Edna Peters, Nellie Beede, Jennie Bullock, Martha Schultz, Helen Beede, Helen Stokes and Marion Bower.

As classes were added to the course of study, more enrolled, space became more cramped, and the land around was sold for building purposes until no space was left for athletics. Early in 1908, the trustees purchased two and one-half acres, and then increased it to 5 acres on A Street across from the park as a site for the high school building. A bond election to raise $20,000 for the building was held in May 1909. Black Diamond claimed it was never consulted about the location of a high school building so they fought the election and the site chosen. The bond election and the petition for a tax levy failed to carry. Soon after, C. A. Hooper of Black Diamond proposed to donate two blocks of land west of the paper mill on the highway landing to Black Diamond. The people of Black Diamond agreed to vote for the bond issue if that site were chosen. Everyone felt that Antioch would surely build that way. The people of Antioch held a meeting and rejected the proposed site and suggested a site in the Hooper tract south of Antioch. This site was refused by the people of Black Diamond.

The question was finally settled by the election for the board of trustees and the location April 1, 1910. The voters chose the location west of Antioch and five trustees in favor of compromising all differences. The money was provided by a direct tax. Since there was no gymnasium, expenses were held within the $20,000 limit. The new high school was not ready until the beginning of the 1911–12 school term.

H. Kittredge was chosen principal of the new building with three teachers. From then on, the high school and grammar school had principals of their own.

The Riverview Union High School building was built to accommodate 120 people. Basketball was played in the library and Club Building (Scouts Hall) or in the Belshaw

View of Antioch taken from the water tower to the southwest. To the right, is the frame school house with its bell. Center left is the Methodist Church, and behind it a bit to the left, is the Holy Rosary Catholic Church. Taken about 1908.

Theatre. The greatest handicap to the school was the lack of a gymnasium, which hampered the whole athletic program. The pupils from Black Diamond, which became Pittsburg in about 1912, continued to pay their own transportation expense. They came mainly by the Santa Fe Railroad. In 1913–14, the trustees provided a bus and gave them free transportation.

Non-curriculum classes began to appear from 1911, one of the first additions being sewing and more commercial courses. Manual training was added in 1912, with cooking in 1913, and music in 1914–15. By 1916, enrollment had reached 130.

Mr. Cater and his shop classes undertook a project of constructing a large shop building northeast of the main building in 1915–16. The new shop building would make it possible for them to use all of their large machinery. The commercial department moved to the basement and in the space recently occupied by the shop classes their program quickly expanded.

The night school program had been held from time to time offering English and civics, mainly for those desirous of becoming citizens. In 1919–20, a large night school program was conducted and included many of the daytime courses. In a few years, the night school attendance decreased, but the demand for English and civics was made, and this part of the program was carried each year.

In 1921, the Antioch-Live Oak grammar school (Fremont) was built for $100,000 and had an enrollment of 700. Bonds had been voted for another grammar school to cost $170,000, to be built in 1926 (John Muir).

Pittsburg experienced continual growth so that in 1922, its people insisted that a branch of the Riverview Union High School stay in Pittsburg. All of their ninth-grade pupils were kept there for instruction during the 1922–23 school term. The following year, they kept the ninth and tenth-grade students. In 1925–25, the eleventh grade remained in Pittsburg. This situation was brought to a head in March 1925, by the election and the suggestion of the dissolution of the Riverview Union.

By a unanimous vote, Antioch petitioned and elected to withdraw from the Riverview Union on June 23, 1925. Pittsburg retained the name of Riverview Union until August, when it became Pittsburg High School.

On July 7, 1925, the Antioch High School District was organized and became Antioch District High School. Antioch continued to use the Riverview School building under the new name. The principal was R. S. Phelps. Antioch-Live Oak Union School District composed of the high school and elementary schools were now under one board of trustees as the school boundaries were identical.

The enrollment steadily increased as shown by the following: 1924–25, 169; 1925–26, 161; 1929–30, 247; 1938–39, 419; 1946–47, 588.

Four teachers of the early 1900s: Miss Mabelle Hust later wrote the early history of the Antioch schools.

The gymnasium construction began in 1926, south of the grammar school (Fremont School). It was occupied in January 1927.

After much complaint and talk in 1927-27 by the citizens, the schools went under a new organization of one executive head, which had not been the case since 1911. Phelps became district superintendent, principal of the high school and supervising principal of the elementary schools.

A plan to construct a new high and junior high school adjacent to the gym and grammar school was started in 1927 by the trustees. The people worked against more taxes and defeated the bill by 65 votes of the two-thirds majority needed. After another attempt and defeat of the same kind of bill, the Parent Teacher Association (P.T.A.) and Mr. Albert Flaherty kept the issue of the need of a new high school always before the people and very much alive. Finally on March 20, 1930, the bill passed, and Antioch was to have a much-needed, larger high school building. The already constructed gym was to serve as the auditorium. The building was completed in 1931 and dedicated October 11, 1931.

Antioch Grammar School about 1895. Mr. Swain, principal; Miss Josie Hawxhurst, teacher. Row one, third from right, Francis Cooney. Row two, fourth from left is the Walrath girl and Ethel Wall at the right end. Row three, first on left is Al Cooney, sixth from left, Emma Bolz Lynn, and to her left is Alda Baker. Row four, first on the left is Paul Stinchfield. Top row, fourth from left is Fred Peters.

In 1936, the district became the Antioch-Live Oak Unified School District. George J. Creary was superintendent and principal of the high school. Mr. Don Cramer was principal of the junior high. Mrs. Leila Sater was principal of the grammar school and Miss Ana Ring was principal of the primary school. The Adult Evening School program was greatly enlarged in 1937, and Cramer became principal.

The old building west of town was leased by the U.S. government in 1935, for use by the Central Valley Conduit Headquarters, the present Research Division of Fibreboard Products, Inc.

Captain Kimball held religious services for the 200 members of his party on the voyage from Boston to San Francisco in 1850. After the arrival of the families in Antioch, Parson Smith held services for the Antioch group at the various homes. At other times, Smith would walk many miles to preach on Sunday to groups around Mt. Diablo and other parts of the county, while the Antioch people would welcome a traveling minister from time to time for a worship service.

High School Completed in 1931 on D Street.

Thomas Gaines by his house at the water front. He was a member of the Congregational Church. Photo taken in 1892.

Antioch's football team in 1910. Standing left to right are, Bedson Juett, Ed Sweeney, Ruel Van Voorbis and Francis Cooney. Seated left to right are, Judson Biglow, Jack Caple, Tony Tellus, Elmer Crawford and Stonewall Glass.

The pioneer church, the First Congregational Church, was founded June 12, 1865. It has functioned continuously since then. Prior to that year, the church had been founded by a young Mr. Morgan, but was short lived. Miss Adelia Kimball founded the Sunday School continuing with it until her marriage in September 1863. She was assisted by the Misses Drusella Boobar and Annie Morrison (Mrs. Joseph Galloway). The Sunday school met in the town hall.

On June 12, 1865, a meeting was conducted in the schoolhouse for all those interested in forming a church. Captain G. W. Kimball acted as chairman, and Reverand J. H. Warren was secretary. A constitution was adopted which, with slight changes and few amendments, is still in force. The members, the first church board of trustees were Joseph Galloway, David Woodruff, G.W. Brown, Captain Kimball and William Utter. The constitution and board were accepted in September 1865.

The first resident pastor Reverend C. Morgan was called later in 1865, at the salary of $1,000 per year. The church was incorporated under state law in 1875, and "The Band of Hope," society for young people was organized and remained active for many years in Antioch.

The Congregational Church was dedicated May 16, 1869. It was razed and the present building at Utter and Kimball (Sixth and F) streets was erected in 1891. This is the oldest church building in Antioch. Its once very graceful, beautiful 40-foot spire atop the belfry had to be removed as a result of the weakening effect of the 1906 earthquake. Reverend W. W. Smith was moderator of the Congregational Church in 1882. The "Parson" would preach from time to time for any church asking him, in the absence of their pastor.

Antioch Grammar School Class of 1912. Miss Hurst was our teacher at this time.

Antioch Baseball Team 1910. Pictured left to right are, Frances Cooney, Ralph Beede, Chas, Bullock, Roscoe Wall, Ferd Stamm, Pete Donlon, Jim Donlon, Ellis Evans, (?) Elmer Martinoni, Al Cooney.

Catholic services were first conducted in 1864, at the John Mulhare home, by Father Vincent Vimpez, O. P. This mission area was served by the Dominican fathers from Benicia, who traveled on horseback.

The first church was built in 1873 on the block between Boobar and Galloway (G and H) on Church (Seventh) Street, the land being donated by Captain Kimball and a Spanish gentleman whose name has been lost.

Father Patrick Callaghan became the first resident priest in 1874. The rectory was built in 1880 for his dwelling. Father Callaghan was succeeded by Father Alphonsus Riley, O. P., in 1902. The beautiful new church was built in 1905, at a cost of $25,000 and was to have been dedicated April 22, 1906. The San Francisco earthquake and fire detained Archbishop Montgomery there to aid with disaster relief. The

Sketch of an unidentified church.

Photo of unidentified church.

Holy Rosary Church was dedicated June 3, 1906. It stood on one of the "highest points of Antioch, at Church (Seventh) and Boobar (G) streets and could easily be discerned from a long distance in whatever direction one approached." The lumber and mill work was done by the Antioch Planing Mill [Editor's note: A planing mill is a lumber mill that smooths and finishes seasoned wood.] and showed a high class of workmanship rarely produced in a town the size of Antioch. The alters and pillars were very artistically designed, and the fact that most of the materials were obtained locally spoke well for the Antioch business standards.

The Christian Advent Church was organized September 25, 1877, by Mrs. M. J. Clark, an evangelist of that denomination, with a charter membership of more than 30, most of whom were at the time members of the Congregational Church. Reverend W. R. Young was the first resident pastor and remained in Antioch off and on, because of ill health, until 1900.

The church, which originally stood on the corner of Marsh (Fourth) and Main (I) streets, was dedicated January 24, 1878. During those early years, the Advent Church welcomed several evangelists of their faith as Dr. Carpenter, Dr. Rogers and Mr. Meeker. They had several semi-annual conferences held in Antioch. The church was moved about 1895, from its original location. By 1920, the church had completely disbanded, its members turning to other churches in the community for membership.

Circuit riders included Antioch in their celebration of the history of Methodism. In September 1868, Noah Burton traveled over the Eden Plain area (Brentwood) and Antioch. He felt Antioch was an unpromising appointment, but had hope for it. In the early 1880s, the Methodists used the Christian Advent Church. The Methodist Church was organized in September 1889. They elected a board of trustees and purchased three lots for $400. They held the first meeting in Homberg Hall under the direction of Reverend James Blackledge. Soon after, Dr. Brill was sent by the State Conference to begin a campaign to raise funds for the purchase of a site. They own the four lots from the corner of Utter and Boobar (Sixth and G) streets, east. Their first church was erected in 1890 for $4,875 and faced Boobar (G) Street. It was dedicated February 8, 1891, by Bishop H.L. Fowler. The parsonage adjoining the church was built in 1892.

The Belshaw Theatre and Store as the building looks today. Photo taken in 1971.

Standing in front of his home is H. W. Baker. Ready for a ride are, from left to right, Frank George and J. Rio Baker. All are wearing Harrison hats.

Methodist Church as it appeared in 1910 facing G at Sixth streets.

Reverend James Williams was then pastor. There was a fire in 1930, and the building was moved to its present location facing Sixth Street and remodeled.

Christian Scientists began to read the lesson sermon at the residence of one of their members in 1910. They rented the Union Hall for midweek and Sunday meetings. The society was organized in July 1911, and in the following year they purchased the lot for their church building at the corner of Fifth and D streets. The temporary chapel building was begun March 1915, at the rear of the lot, facing D Street, leaving room for the main church building when needed. The first meeting occurred in the chapel on April 4, 1915. This building has been redecorated and improved. The chapel is open as a reading room on Tuesday and Friday afternoons.

The Antioch Board of Trade was organized around 1885. It became the Antioch Chamber of Commerce before 1920. Its first officers were as follows: C. W. Belshaw, president; H. F. Beede, vice president; R. Harkinson, treasurer; D. F. Montgomery, secretary-manager. Other members were J. P. Abbott; J. Rio Baker, J. C. Rouse, Dr. Frank Rattan, and Dr. George.

The social and fraternal organizations soon began to appear in the new town and took their place of service, recreation and pleasure, among the Antioch populace.

Antioch Lodge No. 175, F&AM [Editor's note: Free and Accepted Masons] was organized October 12, 1865. The charter members were Francis Williams, Rozwell Hard, J. P. Walton, D. H. Cleaver, Norman Adams, Stephen Jessup, J. J. McNulty, J. C. O'Brien, John E. Wright, Richard Charnock, Jackson W. Ong, Thomas Cryon, and E. T. Mills.

San Joaquin Lodge, No. 151, I.O.O.F. [Editor's note: International Order of Odd Fellows], was instituted January 11, 1869. The charter members were William Girvan, M. S. Levy, George Thyarks, B. Eddy and F. Wildening.

Antioch Lodge, No. 37, A.O.U.W. [Editor's note: Ancient Order of United Workers], was organized by D. D. Barrows in June 1878. The charter members were H.W. Baker, Henry F. Beede, E.L. Wemple, Louis Dahnken, Wm. H. Dohyns, John S. Killicum, L. Meyer, H. J. Breyer, H.C. Wenig and Albert T. Beede.

On the wharf waiting to embark on their boat excursion and picnic are, front row from left, H. F. Beede, Curtis Montgomery, unidentified; Jay Belshaw, ? Meyer, J. T. Belshaw, J. Rouse, R. Harkinson, Dr. George, Frank Wills, Mrs. George behind Dr. and Mrs. Moore. Standing left, Miss Sophie Meyer, unidentified, Mrs. Baler, Mrs. L. Meyer, Miss Mazie Harkinson, J. Rio Baker, Joslin, Mrs. Harkinson, unidentified, Mrs. Pitts, three unidentified. Group of five behind, right to left, unidentified, Mrs. Beede, Charles Montgomery, Mrs. C. M. Belshaw and Mrs. J. Rouse.

Returning for the Centennial celebration in 1951 were natives, seated from left to right are, Jean Baker Turner; Emma Lynn, Dan McKellips, Mary Campbell. Standing are Dr. C. A. Wills, Mrs. Fred Swain, Ramona Cronan, Mrs. Albert Whitfield, Dr. Albert Whitfield.

Ariel Chapter No. 42, O.E.S. [Editor's note: Order of Eastern Star], was organized March 30, 1880. The charter members were Elizabeth Williams, Alice Parkison, Katie E. Forman, Elvina G. Abbott, Alice Louise, Mrs. T. B. Jacobs, Annie. F. McKellips, Alyszan R. Jessup, Mary E. Frink, N. W. Smith, Mary E. Smith, C. H. Frink, G. House, J. P. Abbott.

Young Men's Temperance and Literary Society Association was organized April 8, 1882. The charter members were James Carolan, Charles Smith, R. H. Parkison, Cellus Biglow, John Tope, Frank Biglow, and F. M. Wills.

Good Templars Lodge was organized in December 1882, with 83 charter members.

General Winn Parlor No. 32, Native Sons of the Golden West, was installed July 25, 1884. There were 24 charter members, among them: C. F. Montgomery, president; Frank Robinson, past president; M. C. Hoppe, first vice president; James Carey, second vice president; Richard Uren, third vice president; C. M. Belshaw, R.S.; Charles S. Hardy, F. S.; Eugene Wheelehen, treasurer; R. R. Veale, Jr., marshal; and others: Thomas Griffin, Henry Dahnken, John Wheelehen, Charles Sweeney and Joseph Mulhare.

Antioch Woman's Club was organized February 1902. The founders were Mrs. Mildred A. Meyer (Gabriel), Mrs. Millie G. Abbott, Mrs. Alice V. George, Mrs. Margaret E. Beede (Henry), Mrs. Fannie N. Keeney (C.W.), Mrs. Alice E. Baker (J.R.), Mrs. Juliette C. Harding, Mrs. Sophie Meyer, Mrs. Anna Beede (Ralph), Mrs. Annie J. Hartley, Miss Annie T. McKellips, Mrs. Harkinson, Mrs. Montgomery, Mrs. Moore, and Miss Joslin. The latter four ladies did not become charter members when, in September 1904, the Antioch Club federated with the state and district. The Woman's Clubhouse was made the headquarters for the drive to help those survivors from the San Francisco

Dr. George's Float in the July 4th, 1912 Parade. Lola George, (driving), Frances Whitfield, Nell Beede, Ramona Whitfield, (seated on the side of the car), and Minta Evans. The small boy I am unable to identify.

The Whitfield Family, July 4th, 1909. We were living in the Caple house at this time. Pictured left to right are: Uncle John, my sisters, Frances, Ramona (in the buggy), Mother, Bud (with the dog), Dad Whitfield, Valona Hoey of Martinez, Grandpa Jackson, Lily and her grandmother of San Francisco. President McKinley rode under this flag when he visited San Francisco years ago.

earthquake and fire of April 18, 1906. Antioch offered to care for 100 refugees. Fannie Mason Keeney led the drive for contributions of food and clothing. Shelter was made ready, but the refugees never came for the fire was checked and the people turned to rebuilding their city.

Several Antioch natives were in the City at the time. Senator and Mrs. C. M. Belshaw lived at the St. Francis Hotel, but came to Antioch the day after the "quake." Mr. and Mrs. C. F. Montgomery were guests at the Metropolitan Hotel and watched the outer wall of the hotel fall to the street. Immediately they left. This hotel was later destroyed by fire. Andrew Lauritzen took the *Doris* to San Francisco to help the rescue fleet remove refugees out of San Francisco.

In Antioch the early morning of April 18, 1906, the earthquake was felt, but only a few windows were broken, a few chimneys fell and a few walls cracked. For a week, business was second to the eager gatherings of people to hear news about the quake from the survivors struggling into Antioch.

The public library is a necessary part of any and all growing communities. The first Antioch Library building was built in 1917, by funds raised by a committee consisting of Mrs. Mary Fulton, Mrs. C. W. Keeney and Mrs. H. A. West. The lot on the corner of Sixth and F streets was purchased with the Carnegie Corporation Endowment. Many attempts were made toward a library prior to 1917. Among the first were the reading rooms for members established by the Young Men's Temperance and Literary Society and then by the Good Templars.

After Scouts Hall was built, Mr. Williams made reading rooms in the front. In 1911, the Woman's Club organized a library association, assessed each member $1 per year and as many books as they could spare from their private shelves. Their club room became the reading room. The county library system was first formed in 1913, and the local library association began immediate cooperation and began free circulation of the books allotted to Antioch by the county. Since that time, the people of Antioch have had access to practically any book printed on any subject. By being a member of

Grammar School Class of 1893. Anyone for identification?

Antioch's first library building endowed by the Carnegie Fund. It is located on F at Sixth streets. Photo taken in 1971.

the Contra Costa library system, any book needed for reference or study, not in Antioch, can be requested from the Congressional Library in Washington, D.C.

Scouts Hall was built at the corner of Third and F streets, next to the G. W. Kimball home. George M. Williams came to Antioch in 1905. After consulting with several leading citizens and his friend John Barnhurst, minister of the Methodist Church, he decided to build a house for the use of the young people of Antioch. Scouts Hall was the result. The front was to be a library and the back a gymnasium. After 1917, the library was moved. The Boy Scouts used the hall. In 1920, Mr. Williams decided to convert the building into apartments, as places to live were in demand. It was renamed San Joaquin Apartments. The building was built in the Grecian manner, with Doric columns and a wide portico.

The Antioch Hotel, location of the later Arata Building. Now the Townhouse. Photo taken in 1971.

Boy Scout Encampment, Beede's Bungalow, Marsh Landing, 1909. Dr. George, scout master; Mr. Earl, assistant. This was quite a group of lads.

Scouts Hall (left), located at the corner of Third at F streets. It was later remodeled and became the San Joaquin Apartments (right). Front and west-side view. Photo taken in 1951.

Of interest always are recipes. Maybe some of these from the *California Recipe Book of 1872*, Brice Printing House, San Francsico, used in Antioch would be of interest to you.

CAKE: The cake should be put in the oven as soon as made. Be very accurate in proportioning the ingredients. The oven being already hot, and ready for it. The eggs must be fresh and the butter good. Do not leave the eggs or butter in tin, as the coldness of the latter prevents the lightness of the cake. To ascertain if the cake is sufficiently done, use a straw; if it comes out the least moist, let the cake remain in the oven longer.

SALT-PORK CAKE: One pound of pork, chopped very fine, 1 cup of warm water, 1 cup of sugar, 1 cup of molasses, 1 teaspoon of soda, 4 eggs, spice, raisins and citron.

CALF'S HEAD: Tie up the brains in muslin, with sweet herbs; put them into the pot with the head and the haslet, without the liver, and boil two hours, keeping it more that covered with water. Put in the liver for the last hour. When nearly done, take up the brains and part of the lights, chop them up with a hard-boiled egg, add a little butter, season with pepper and salt, add a little of the broth, strew in a little flour and stew it up a little to make a nice sauce. Take up the rest of the meat, clean it from the bones, lay it on a dish and spread over the sauce. Thicken and season the water for broth, in which an onion and a little rice have been boiled.

Home Bakery delivery cart driven by Dick Hopkins, whose father operated the bakery.

STRIPED BASS: Disliked by many as usually cooked, would be more generally approved if cooked long enough. Three hours are required to boil or bake a large bass.

SCRAMBLED EGGS: Two great spoonfuls of milk, put into a stew pan. When ready to boil, add six eggs, well beaten. When nearly done, add a piece of butter, and a little salt. Stir quickly all the time.

ISINGLASS BLANC MANGE: Two ounces of isinglass [Editor's note: a kind of gelatin or collegen obtained from fish]; three pints of milk, one-half pound sugar, lemon. Boil 5 minutes. Pour into a serving dish. Cool and serve.

GREEN CORN CAKES:1 pint of green corn, 3 tea cups of milk, 1 do. [Editor's note: a "do." is an abbreviation for "dollop"- a unit of measurement equivalent to 1 tablespoon of soft food.] of flour. 2 tablespoons of butter, 1 egg, a little salt and pepper. Fry in small cakes on a griddle.

POP-OVERS: 3 eggs, 3 cups milk, 3 do. of flour; bake in cups half full, or gem pans, a little salt.

PASTRY AND PIES: Pastry should be used as soon as made, as it is better fresh than after being kept a day or two. For a good common pie-crust looks nicer made of lard; but tastes better half butter. Rub one-half of your shortening, well, with two-thirds of your flour adding a little salt; then add sufficient cold water to make it sufficiently moist to roll out; spread on the reserve shortening as you roll it out, sprinkling on the reserved flour.

Part III   Educational, Spiritual and Social Life   75

View of Antioch about 1910. Extreme left, from bottom to top are the Bullock, Cooney and Belshaw homes. Top to center left, the smoke stack for the paper company. Top right Arlington Hotel, Ross Store immediately in front. Across the street is the Donlon Ice and Fuel on the corner of Third and G streets. Center right is the Keeney home and barn and right bottom is the McGrath home.

Looking from the water tower northeast to the river. Lower left to right, homes on Fourth Street are 1. Center can be seen to the left, the back of the Scouts Hall, then the Kimball home and the Schott home. Beyond town the river can be seen as can the lumber company office and the planing mill and numerous boats on the river. Photo taken about 1910.

Always of interest has been the River-For-Fun, Swimming-beach area where Fulton Shipyards stands today. Looking from the river toward the beach.

LEMON TARTS: Grind rind of two lemons, juice of one lemon, piece of about the size of an egg, one egg, sugar to taste. Simmer all together till thick. Bake puffs (pie crust shells) and fill while hot. Makes 30 tarts. They refer to using the whites of eggs beaten, as frosting.

PUDDING BAGS: Should be made of thick, close sheeting to exclude the air. Before using them, they should be wrung out in hot water, then thoroughly floured on the inside. In typing, leave room to swell. A place in the bottom of the pot prevents the bag from burning. Keep the pudding covered with water and do not let it stop boiling. If necessary, fill up the pot with hot, but never cold water.

BOILED INDIAN PUDDING: 1½ quarts of milk, 1 pint of meal. Boil the milk, stir in the meal gradually. Take it from the fire, add 4 or 5 eggs, sugar and syrup to taste, pretty sweet. Boil in a cloth for 2 or 3 hours. To be eaten with butter.

COFFEE: Put a large coffee-cupful into a pot that will hold three pints of water; add the white of an egg, or a few shavings of isinglass [Editor's note: a kind of gelatin or collagen obtained from a fish], or a well-cleansed and dried bit of fish skin of the size of a 10 cents piece. Pour upon it boiling water and boil it five or six minutes. Then pour a gill [Editor's note: 4 ounces] from the spout, in order to remove it, and pour it back into the pot. Let it stand eight or 10 minutes, where it will keep hot, but not boil; boiling coffee a great while makes it strong, but not so lively or agreeable. If you have no cream, boil a saucepan of milk, and after pouring it into the pitcher, stir it now and then, till the breakfast is ready, that the cream may not separate from the milk, make coffee stronger or weaker as you prefer, by using a larger or smaller measure of ground coffee.

Part III Educational, Spiritual and Social Life 77

Looking from the beach toward the river.

POISON OAK: And perhaps you have wanted to cure poison oak! Try this. Dissolve 1 ounce of gum-shellac in 6 ounces of sulfuric ether; work tightly in a bottle. Bathe the surface where the irritation or eruption appears with cold water and wipe dry, then apply the above solution. The ether will evaporate in one minute, leaving an elastic coating of gum, completely impervious to the air. In about 2 minutes, the most distressing case of poison oak can be relieved entirely of all unpleasant sensations. As the coating cracks or peels off, apply more of the solution, and in 24 hours the case of indescribable suffering is completely healed.

Bummers Corner 1892. Pictured from left to right, Judge J. P. Abbott, R. Harkinson, Uncle Billy Forman, Charles Montgomery and Collins Brown. The bench was located at the west wall of the Brown and Baker Hardware Store.

Second Congregational Church Building, located at Sixth and F streets. Photo taken in 1971.

Masons and Odd Fellows Cemetery east of Antioch as it appears in 1971.

Antioch Woman's Club on G Street between Fifth and Sixth streets. Photo taken in 1971.

Arata Grocery on Second Street Between H and I streets.

West view of Hickmott Cannery. Photo taken in 1971.

Part III Educational, Spiritual and Social Life 79

Residence of Hon. C. M. Belshaw.

Residence of Dr. W. S. George.

Nelson Peterson home built about 1880, located on the north side of Third Street between G and H streets. Photo taken in 1951.

Remfree, corner of E and Sixth streets. Photo taken in 1971.

Donlon home moved from the northern corner of G and Third streets to the north side of Third between G and H streets, Photo taken in 1951.

Hayes - Fourth between E and F streets.

Worrel - Southeast corner of Sixth and G streets. Built before 1890.

House on the south side of Sixth between E and F streets. Builder and early occupants are unknown. Photo taken in 1971.

Waldie - Corner of Eighth and D streets. Home built by the grandfather of Congressman Jerome Waldie. Photo taken in 1971.

Cooney home located on the south side of Fourth between E and F streets. Photo taken in 1951.

Part III Educational, Spiritual and Social Life 81

T. N. Wills, Nash - Ninth Street between C and D streets. Rebuilt in 1871. Photo taken in 1951.

S. K. McKellips - northwest corner of Sixth and F streets. Built in 1886.

Carman house as it appeared in 1876; lower right, same home as it appeared in 1951.

Charles Marsh, Hartley - Southwest corner of Fourth and G streets. Built in 1887; upper right corner, 1951.

J. T. Belshaw - Southeast corner of Fourth and G streets.

Galloway, Rouse home located at First Street between G and H streets. About 1890.

G. W. Kimball home as it appeared after 1910 until it was torn down in 1956. Photo taken in 1951.

J. P. Abbott home at the corner of Third and E streets. Photo taken in 1951.

Hawxhurst home at the corner of Fifth and C streets about 1890. Photo taken in 1951.

Pitts home at the corner of Second and F streets. Photo taken in 1951.

Harkinson home at the northeast corner of Fourth and D streets, about 1890. Photo taken in 1951.

Ferd Stamm home, B Street between Fifth and Sixth streets. Photo taken in 1951.

Home of John Thomas Cox on the south side of Sixth Street between B and C streets. Photo taken in 1971.

Dr. DeWitt home at I Street between Third and Fourth streets. Photo taken in 1951.

Wilkening, Thyarks home at the southwest corner of Ninth and D streets. Photo taken in 1951.

Mason, Keeney home at the northeast corner of Fourth and G streets; built before 1900. Photo taken in 1951.

Part III   Educational, Spiritual and Social Life   83

Mason, Brown, Ralph Beede home at the southeast corner of Sixth and D streets. About 1890. Photo taken in 1970.

G. Meyer home at Fifth Street, between D and E streets. Photo taken in 1951. Mike and Catherine Benyo, lower right.

M. Belshaw, corner of Seventh and E streets, about 1890. Photo taken in 1970.

Dr. Wemple, Dr. Rattan barn at the southwest corner of Tenth and E streets. Photo taken in 1951.

Heath home at the southwest corner of Sixth and G streets. Photo taken in 1951.

Azevedo home at Sixth Street between F and G streets. Photo taken in 1951.

One house built by J. Rio Baker. Recent home of Jean Baker Turner. F Street between Seventh and Eighth streets. Photo taken in 1970.

Priests' residence at Old Catholic Church 1890; moved to Eighth Steet between F and G streets. Made into two flats. Photo taken in 1951.

Four houses built in 1904 by the Field brothers, H Street between Fourth and Fifth streets. Photo taken in 1970.

Riverview Union High school Band.

Part IV

Farming, Produce and Climate

As with any new settlement, far from other settlements, farming was a necessity for life. The people of Antioch soon found the rich, fertile soil would yield a bountiful harvest when cared for properly. The climate was mild enough to allow the growth of many tropical and semitropical fruits and vegetables and still cool enough to allow for the growth of the produce of the temperate and colder climates.

Farming soon took its place as a principal industry of Antioch. It kept Antioch alive when the shipping of coal was diverted to other points around 1870. These early years showed these people that one of their best means of livelihood was the raising and shipping of the farm produce to the regions of denser population where farming was becoming impossible. These people soon learned that the various vegetables could be planted and grown the year 'round.

As early as 1867, many families became interested in raising silkworms. The mulberry trees, food of the silkworms, were planted. The worms flourished, but the people soon learned what a tedious job silkworm culture was and gave up the project after a few years. Some of the mulberry trees are still to be found around Antioch.

For a while, peanuts were quite an important crop of the Antioch region, many of the farms being located on the islands.

The outstanding agricultural regions of today were soon discovered by the early settlers and are Lone Tree, Live Oak, Oakley, Knightsen, Brentwood, and Byron. These are all embodied in the Diablo Valley, and it forms more than 8,000 acres of the rich Delta region, generally spoken of as a triangle with Sacramento, Stockton and Antioch as the three points. [Editor's note: the heart of today's Sacramento-San Joaquin Delta Heritage Area.] Today, to drive east or southeast from Antioch is to soon be in part of the richest agricultural producing regions of California.

In the early years, produce was sent or received at such points as Babbe Landing in the Knightsen area. Iron House Landing is again in the Knightsen area but north of Babbe. Marsh Landing was in the area where the PG&E steam plant now stands. Smith's Point was the point of land just west of Fulton Shipyard of today.

Ferry *Francis* carrying passengers and produce between Stockton and Antioch.

A harvesting scene in 1894 on (No. 40) the Frank McFarlon ranch. Steam-powered threshing machine generated power by using water on the wagon at its left and by burning the straw in front of it. Page 79. [Editor's note: sic.]

Dr. Marsh set a claim to 800 acres of land just outside of Antioch. It extended from East (A) Street to Bridgehead on Wilbur Avenue and another parcel of 300 acres extending from the Holy Cross Cemetery to Bridgehead Road and to the river. This property came into Mr. Roundtree's possession after it had been taken from Dr. Marsh. In 1869, Manuel Viera rented it for an annual rental of 10 cents an acre. Roundtree was never heard from again when he departed for the mines, so the county sold it after 4 years.

They sold it to the Peabody interests of New York for the taxes. Mr. Viera held squatter's rights which he sold for $1 to Mr. I. R. Wilbur (Wilbur Avenue was named for him), the agent of Peabody's to make it legal. Mr. Viera continued to rent, though he could have gotten the land for 50 cents per acre. He later bought considerable acreage.

In 1868, Mr. and Mrs. John Whelihan (parents of Mrs. Manuel Viera) came and purchased a farm, one-half-mile south of the Community Cemetery, from the railroad. The property of "Frenchman" Whelihan adjoined the Whelihan property. West of Whelihan ranch was that of Tom Uren, uncle of T. H. Uren. The McQuade ranch was the present residential property between Hillcrest Road and Cavallo and from Cavallo Road to East (A) Street across to Tregallas.

Early settlers of Sherman Island and the farming land east of Antioch on Wilbur Avenue were the Biglows, A. Judson and brother Pharcellus K., who moved from Sacramento to Sherman Island. They were pioneers in raising early rose potatoes, asparagus, planting grapes, apricots and peaches.

Lone Tree Way had a landmark in the 1870s of a huge oak tree, thus the name. The tree stood on the county road and on the Loreyea ranch. It was sold to Frank Smith in 1910. On this road was the ranch of John Fitzpatrick, and to the east was the home of Jack Bonnickson, who later took over the adjoining property of the Tom Wallace family. To the south was the Jim Fitzpatrick farm. To the north is the property held and operated by the Davidson family for three generations. West of the Davidson place was the Oak Springs ranch which was owned by Hans Jensen. It was later owned by the Aratas.

The Somersville Road was the location for several farms. They were Tom Tormey (Frank S. Arata's), just east of this, the John Kerns farm (Prewitt interests operated by the Ginocchio family).

Almond harvest.

Jim O'Hara brought the almond industry to the area in 1900. He was often called the father of the industry. He bought a section of land across from where the old O'Hara home was, near Oakley. He cleared it of grubby trees and chaparral, as was necessary of all newcomers. He broke the heavy growth with a roller and burned the brush. Then he used a single plough drawn by a 5-horse team to bring up all the shrub and tree roots which were gathered and burned.

The tender, year-old almond trees were planted. The trunk of each tree was carefully wrapped with paper. All the young trees were further protected by a 3-foot wire netting fence to keep out the numerous rabbits which delighted in eating the tender almond leaves, and when the leaves were too high, ate the bark.

The Bridgehead area in the 1890s saw the Diethelms and Ruckstuhls settling just east of Bridgehead. The Ruckstuhl brothers were later known for their winery. The John Rhamm holding south of the other two properties is another old estate purchased from the Flackhammers. South to the "hill ranches" where hay and grain were the crops, were found the Peter Harris ranch and the adjoining ranch of the original Brun family.

Much of this property was first bought for $5 an acre, but when it was sold in smaller lots, the price was $60 an acre.

Around Antioch, we find four types of soil existing in the Diablo Valley. They are:

1. The residual soil of the hill, pasture and range land.
2. The old alluvial soil, which is a moderately heavy clay loam extending from Bay Point to Antioch producing hay and grain.

3. The recent alluvial soil ranging from Oakley sand to Yolo clay loam, found through the Oakley, Antioch, Brentwood and Byron sections.
4. The rich peat soil of the fertile Delta section.

To summarize the produce of the latter two soils would be to say that in the recent alluvial soil, the lighter soil crops include almonds, apricots, peaches and grapes. The intermediate soil crops are walnuts, grain, peaches, tomatoes and apricots. The heavy soil crops are hay, grain and alfalfa. The soils adapt very well to pears, plums and prunes. The rich peat soil of the Delta islands produces celery, onions, beans, sugar beets, asparagus and record crops of the grains.

The Delta lands were formed by deposits of sediments washed down from the uplands of the Sierra Nevada and the eastern slope of the Coastal Range.

Peat is the result of the decomposition of plant growth in the presence of water. This partially carbonized vegetable material, peat, mixed with the silts brought down by the river waters, forms the rich Delta land of today. It is of two types, sedimentary loams and nearly pure peat.

The rich farming land of the Delta created a long course of reclamation and development. The many water channels have been deepened by dredging and by the construction of levees. Great clamshell dredges were used during the earlier period of reclamation. Their hulls were 140-feet long, and they had a beam of 60 feet. From them, booms with a 200-foot swing-out manipulated clamshell buckets of 5-cubic-yard capacity. The work still goes on, but much smaller dredges serve. It is a constant job to keep up the levees and smaller canals. The drainage district does the work, and it is subscribed to regularly by the landowners.

Members of the threshing crew with the bags of grain harvested about 1894. Front row from left to right: Bill Sullenger, Parlman Biglow, John Canssi, Manuel Viera, Tip Welch, Frank Rafitt. Back row from left: Fred Jessie, Joe Rose, ? Tony Xavier, Joe Fraga, another Joe Fraga, Andy Benson, Robert Noia, Nels Broad, John F. Viera, ?, Johnny Lawrence. The two standing are unidentified.

This picture was taken in 1904 near the top of the hill by the (No. 41) old Brentwood Coal Mine. Left to right: Frank Records, Joe G. Viera, Gilbert Musselman, John F. Viera, Sr., and Frank Wehie. John operated the rig and knew well the names of the 32 horses and mules pulling the rig.

The irrigation of the Delta lands is by a unique system. Crops are sub irrigated, never flooded. Under a natural head of 3 feet, the water is syphoned through 6-inch pipes into a main irrigation canal, which crosses the field as the topography indicates. From this main canal, smaller lateral ditches lead off, cutting the tract into long rectangles of 20 to 40 acres in area. From these laterals at spaced intervals of 50 to 75 feet, smaller ditches extend, these being less than 1-foot wide and 30-inches deep. This system of ditches distributes the water over the entire area by gravity. Pumping is necessary when drainage is to be done. Pumps are installed at the lower end of the main channels. They are driven by electric motors of gas engines and send the water over the levee into the nearest river channel.

We notice that in 1853, John C. O'Brien purchased cattle and engaged in stock raising and later farming. In the same year, Robert R. Fuller took up agricultural pursuits and settled on a 160-acre farm adjoining Antioch. In 1857, William F. Forman engaged in farming 8 miles east of Antioch, but later moved to Antioch.

In 1868, T. M. Wills moved to Antioch and purchased 280 acres of land adjoining Antioch to the south and engaged in farming. His home was built on Knapp (Ninth) Street in 1871 and overlooked his land extending back to the now Fitzuren Road. Amos M. Graves purchased 160 acres 2 miles east of Antioch, engaging in farming. One of the finest contributions made to farming was a successful experiment made by the Honorable A. G. Darby, who settled on a 320-acre farm in the Lone Tree Valley in 1869, 6 miles southwest of Antioch. Though grain raising was his chief business, he worked with fruit, nut and forest trees. He found that the almond was good for the driest seasons, taking very deep root. His experiment was the finding of the great advantage in budding peach shoots on almond roots. This proved to be a great benefit during the dry seasons. During these early years, the islands Sherman,

William and Kimball were very important centers for the raising of crops and dairying. The Hiram Hills farm was in the Lone Tree Valley.

When J. C. Preston came to the Point of Timber area in 1865, there were few settlers, with none of the country improved. There was scarcely a hose between his place and Antioch, which was the nearest post office, 15 miles away.

The land was supposed to be too dry and sandy to produce a crop without irrigation. By deep plowing and summer fallowing, the land produces the best of crops. In 1865, Preston put in 40 acres of wheat and got 40 bushels to the acre. He got as much as 80 bushels per acre in later years. Scattering grain at harvesting was ample planting for the next year without plowing.

Josiah Wills came to California in 1871, with only about $800. He bought a small tract of land and began farming in the Lone Tree area in 1872. He later bought 320 acres of land. The Central Pacific Railroad passed through his ranch, bringing it within 2 hours of San Francisco. His land, just 6 miles from Antioch, had been considered almost useless because it was too dry and sandy. He had an orchard, fruit, flowers and raised some good crops of grain. He said that by proper cultivation and management, as good crops could be raised on his farm as anywhere in the state.

Mr. Sellers near "Iron House" Landing, set out a large field of mulberry trees. These made fine-quality leaves for the silkworms. A house was fitted up for a feeding room for the worms and business proved successful. In 1878, Mrs. Sellers exhibited cocoons and silkworms at the County Fair. She was also experimenting with methods of making silk. Two crops of cocoons were raised in a year, in May and July, the time when the weather was best suited to the delicate silkworms and when there was least danger to the mulberry leaf.

The State of California, with the hope of establishing the silk-making business as one of its fixed incomes, offered $250 for every 5,000 mulberry trees, payment to be made when the trees were 2 years old; also, a $300 payment for every 100,000 cocoons. The business did not prove profitable because of the lack of capital and people with time to give to the constant care of the worms.

A news item of June 30, 1906 read, "the big dredger *Tule Queen* passed by Antioch up the river Monday night, bound for Union Island to endeavor to close a 300-foot break in the levee where Middle River is pouring a flood of water over a vast acreage of valuable crops."

Also, of the same date we note, "... that R. Hickmott of San Francisco was in Antioch Wednesday, having returned from a trip to Bouldin Island where he reports no water on the island and everything in good condition.

An earlier news report read, "Kimball Island owned by Captain Kimball has been reclaimed for years and has withstood the high waters. Nearly every kind of grain and vegetable, as well as first-class fruit trees, were raised on the island."

The G. W. Kimball home east view showing the earthen-floored room. The tree is one of the mulberry trees planted to encourage the silk industry. Photo taken before 1900.

The Antioch pioneers soon learned that with a few exceptional years as 1851, when drought killed the plant life, that the climate was exceptionally fine. Since 1878, when the weather records were started, Antioch's average annual maximum temperature is 74.5 degrees, and the annual minimum is 47.5 degrees. The temperature is not extreme in any degree. The record shows that rain falls in Antioch, 11 of the 12 months, with most of it coming from November through April. From May through October, the average annual rainfall is 1.39 inches. July and August are the dry months. July shows only a trace of rain and August only .01 of an inch. January averages the wettest month with 2.67 inches. The records show an average of only 42 rainy days per year. The yearly rainfall average is 12.65 inches. The recorded maximum rainfall was in 1940–41 with 22.29 inches while the minimum rainfall came in 1946 with 6.81 inches. There was a July day in the last 50 years when the thermometer rose to 114 degrees and a night in December during the same period when the thermometer dropped to 14 degrees. These extremes make for the interest and the sparkling conversation.

Old timers of Antioch were said to watch the shift in the wind to determine when rain would come. A wind from the south or southeast shifting to the southwest is a sure indication of rain.

The fog is remembered by many. As one old timer put it, "Fog, why it was so thick, I had to use the coal railroad tracks to keep me going straight as I couldn't see my hand at arms' length in front of my face."

Even on the hottest day in Antioch, there is a breeze sweeping up from the ocean and San Francisco Bay. It keeps the community from the real heat of the central valleys. The Japanese current that modifies the winter temperatures of the Bay region, helps Antioch to be modified and miss the freezing temperatures of the interior. There is February 1873, when snow was very low in the foothills and would have fallen on parts of the present Antioch. New Year's Eve of 1882, saw snow commence to fall just before noon and continuing all afternoon, evening, night and well into January 1, 1883. There is the snow that fell Christmas afternoon of 1946, but melted as soon as it touched the ground. Of course, we must not forget the hail storm of March 1951, varying in depth according to the location, but giving the children a chance to make snowmen many of them playing in the snow-hail found in shady and sheltered places, for two days afterward.

Antioch is located on the south bank of the San Joaquin River about 3 miles from the point where it converges with the Sacramento River. Antioch is 39 miles east of Oakland, 39 miles west of Stockton, 47 miles from San Francisco and 54 miles south of Sacramento. The elevation varies from almost 15 feet at City Hall, to an average of 30 feet above sea level. The ground gradually slopes upward to the

Beede country home located east of A Street just south of Tenth Street. About 1895.

south from the bank of the river with fairly flat terrain for a mile and one-half. Then the broadly terraced slopes merge into rolling foothills, which become quite steep as the base of Mt. Diablo has an elevation of 3,849 feet and is the Base Meridian used by the U.S. Coast and Geodetic Survey.

An important economic factor to Antioch must be kept in mind when considering the agricultural production of the Antioch region. Crops are planted, harvested and shipped during every month of the year.

Henry F. Beede country home as it appears in 1971.

In a report of Contra Costa County agriculture of 1872 appears the following:

Land enclosed - 125,940 acres
Land cultivated - 69,790 acres

PRODUCT	ACRES	HARVESTED
Wheat	51,140	701,720 Bushels
Barley	15,400	310,030 Bushels
Oats	1,800	48,900 Bushels
Rye	670	2,000 Bushels
Corn	200	5,320 Bushels
Buckwheat	30	570 Bushels
Peas	204	10 Bushels
Beans	225	4,560 Bushels
Onions	28	3,810 Bushels
Potatoes	90	16,890 Tons
Hay	13,700	14,300 Tons
Beets	—	1,800 Tons
Sweet potatoes	6	30 Tons

The area around Antioch contributed considerably to the totals of the above table. In 1884, ships loaded wheat at Antioch in one week.

In 1891, the county's acreage was planted as follows:

Wheat	44,500 acres
Barley	28,400 acres
Corn	2,200 acres
Oats	1,600 acres

The use of the Delta-Diablo area for vegetable production brought vegetable growing for commercial purposes into volume for the county.

Fruit soon became very important in the county. Pears became the largest fruit crop in Contra Costa County. Many unusual or odd fruits were also grown, including persimmons, loquats, pomegranates, nectarines, guavas and kumquats.

Asparagus has long been known in Antioch. It was planted on the islands by the Kimballs, later planted in the tule land by the Biglows, east of Antioch. It was not until Bill Meek shipped the first asparagus to eastern markets, that Antioch became the first well-known shipping center, and the Delta became a major asparagus producer. It is a known fact that in 1926, the San Joaquin Delta region had 15,249 acres in asparagus. The Delta region raised 90 percent of the world's asparagus with Antioch as the principal shipping point. In the 1920s and later, Antioch shipped more than 250 railway carloads of fresh asparagus, valued at $500,000 to distant markets. The first shipments of the fresh "grass" (well-known nickname for asparagus) were made on the following days of the indicated years: for 1922, March 24; 1923, March 19; 1924, February 24; 1925, February 18. Much of the fresh "grass" was sent by American Railway Express.

A newspaper article of February 1906, states:

> A building is being erected near the wharf on the asparagus cannery property, which will be used as a cold storage plant. The "grass" often arrives from the fields late in the evening and just wait until morning to be canned. When it is not canned at once, it loses some of its freshness. Last year, it was found that by chilling, it retained all of the crispness and flavor as when first cut. The cold storage building will ensure the "grass" remaining in fine condition until canned.

Another article in March 1906, states:

> More interest is being given the asparagus industry each year. Theories have been advanced from time to time as to the soil best adapted to its cultivation. There is no doubt but that the rich tule land produces as fine a product as can be grown, but it can be successfully grown in the sand lands. Also, Manuel Roche, a rancher living about three miles east of Antioch, has been experimenting for some time in growing asparagus and last May planted about three-quarters of an acre in sand. He has already begun to cut from the beds which are less than 10 months old. The growth is remarkable for such a short time, many of the stalks of "grass" measure an inch in diameter.

Asparagus is a very profitable crop for the farmer. The roots are purchased and planted 2 years before they produce the desired crop. They continue to yield for 15 years. The Delta Islands grow most of the enormous annual crop which is shipped and canned in a large percent from Antioch. There is "grass" grown in the tule lands and the sand lands between Antioch and Oakley.

Asparagus has become a generally used vegetable, containing a rich source of vitamins, protein, sugars and phosphoric acid salts. It is canned in large quantities and shipped to all parts of the United States and the world. Over the period of years, the number of carloads of fresh asparagus is decreasing while the canned "grass" is increasing. In 1924, 269 carloads of fresh "grass" compared to 55 carloads in 1951, were shipped, while only 47 carloads of canned were shipped in 1924, compared with 500 carloads of canned shipped in 1950. By 1924, the R. Hickmott Canning Company was packing in cans some 38,000 cases of asparagus each year under the labels of "Signature," "R. H." "Golden Crown," "El Captain," "Silver Crescent," and "Perfection." Today, besides the Hickmott Company, the Western California Canners of Antioch increase the yearly output of canned asparagus.

Scene from eastern Antioch soutwest to the hills.

Celery is another very large and important product of the Delta with large shipments from Antioch. In 1923, Antioch shipped 1,628 cars of celery with a valuation of $814,000 from 3,320 acres planted.

Other staple food products of the Delta are potatoes, onions, corn, beans, sugar beets and the grains. The Delta farmers are credited with approximately 15 percent of the nation's annual production of vegetables. The Delta region plants 25,000 acres of potatoes each year and yields two-thirds of the California potato crop. Potato shipment from Antioch ran around 500 cars per season in the 1920s.

Truck gardening was a new venture of the Diablo Valley where by 1925, interplanting between the growing young orchard trees was giving excellent returns from squash, peppers, beans, cucumbers, cabbage, corn, persian, [Editor's note: persian is a variety of small, seedless cucumber.] honeydew and other melons, lettuce and tomatoes. More than 800 acres planted in tomatoes with daily shipments reaching 1,000 boxes. The value of the 1925 tomato crop was more than $75,000. Three times the acreage of the 1925 crop was signed up for the 1926 planting.

The first interplanting of eggplant was made in 1925 by Carl O'Brien. It was such a success that it became an important annual crop.

Rhubarb was introduced into the Lone Tree district in 1922. It proved to be a profitable crop, easy to grow with not much care. The Lone Tree district was used mainly for dry farming and pasture purposes, until irrigation, then introduced, revolutionized the farming of that region. The varieties of new orchards are unlimited: peaches, apricots, pears, grapes, and cherries intermingled with vegetables. There are around 2,000 acres in this district appearing as a garden.

Alfalfa is a crop of major importance purchased under irrigation in the Byron-Bethany, Knightsen and Lone Tree Irrigation districts. Six to eight crops per year with 6 to 8 tons of good-quality hay as an average crop on the Delta Islands we find 18,823 acres in alfalfa in 1924. In the Diablo Valley, the alfalfa

Waterfront - showing one of many ships that called at the Antioch wharves to unload supplies and load the many products of the area.

crop of 1824, was valued at more than $1 million. In 1925, the first cutting of alfalfa was shipped from the valley May 7. Alfalfa is considered an intermediate crop between grain and orchards. It increases the fertility of the soil for orchards. Much of the alfalfa land of the 1920s is now in orchards in the Diablo Valley.

Grain (wheat, barley, corn, rye) is grown in large amounts, mostly in the regions not under irrigation. The shipment of grain from the Diablo Valley in 1924, amounted to 53 carloads. In the Delta for the same year there were 21,103 irrigated grain acres and 59,630 dry farming acres of grain.

Apricots are a very important fruit crop of the Antioch region. They are shipped fresh, canned or dried. The absence of brown rot is a very important fact in making apricots such an important fruit crop. In 1925, Diablo Valley shipped 66,000 boxes of fresh apricots to Eastern markets. Oakley, and since irrigation, the Lone Tree districts are the most successful apricot regions. The "cot" received from $80 to $115 per ton on the New York market in the 1920s.

The Oakley region has another variety of crop more often associated with the Old World, the olive. It is generally used for border planting.

Many fruits raised around Antioch have the advantage over other regions, for they ripen and are ready for market first, thus commanding the highest prices in the Eastern markets. The first Mayflower peaches of the season were shipped from the Diablo Valley May 21, 1925. While the first strawberries were ripe in the same region April 8, 1925. Figs were introduced for commercial purposes around 1922. They are excellent producers and the young orchards of the California Black Fig and the Kodota varieties showed unusual quality.

Grapes have for years been a very important crop, the juice and the table varieties are both in demand, though the latter varieties became commercially important since 1922. The juice grapes grown around

Oakley have 20 to 25 percent more sugar than the wine grapes grown elsewhere in California, thus they bring around $20 more per ton. The table variety of grapes are the Tokay, particularly the Flame Tokay. By 1926, Mr. C. B. Douglass near Antioch, had ample proof of the adaptability of this variety, having regularly shipped the first Tokay grapes in the state.

Mr. Tom Milan, of Antioch, on his 20-acre tract in the Lone Tree district harvested in 1925, three tons of Tokay grapes per acre, from three-year-old vines. It is conservative to say that a season's picking will net this region 7,500 tons of grapes.

Almonds are one of the oldest commercial crops of the Oakley-Antioch district. These orchards are the first to bloom in the spring and gives to the countryside, a beauty and fairyland appearance enjoyed year after year by all who can drive to see it. The almonds are subject to variations in production, but are as dependable here as in any district. The quality is excellent. In 1923, this region shipped 39 carloads of almonds.

Walnuts are considered one of the later crops, not coming into prominence until around 1924. Before this time, the trees had been used as border planting. The old trees are well-scattered but the larger plantings show good adaptability to the region. The Concord walnut is one of the leading varieties.

Climate, soil and nearness to market helped advance the poultry industry since the 1920s when only a few commercial poultry ranches were in existence compared to the vaster representation of the industry today.

Some of the early successful poultrymen were W. W. Hammond, Vanderbundt Brothers and G. Somerhalder. Poultry raising increased as it brings in some income throughout the year, which is important to any farm and a necessity on smaller holdings.

Stock raising, beef cattle, sheep and hogs have been important to the survival of Antioch and the Diablo Valley since the first settler, John Marsh arrived in 1836. The hilly land is better adapted to grazing

Antioch from the south hills. Photo taken in 1970.

View of the hills to the south from Antioch. Note Mt. Diablo in the distance.

than anything else. The number of sheep in the irrigated regions has increased since the 1920s. Both the beef and sheep farmers do very well. These animals are easily sold to the nearby markets. There are a few goats found in this district and are more and more in demand for their milk.

It is interesting to note that in 1923, the following shipments were made from the Diablo Valley: Cattle, 29 carloads; hogs, 56 carloads; and sheep, 136 carloads. The Department of Commerce, Washington D. C., reports the following statistics on livestock in the Diablo Valley in 1925: Horses, 5,534; mules, 420; beef cows, 6,023; other beef cattle, 7,196; dairy cows, 8,626; other dairy cattle, 2,079; hogs, 2,674.

Water has always been one of the most important issues in Antioch. From the first, the settlers realized that to survive meant the irrigation of crops. The Pulsifer Brothers used a form of home-made pump to irrigate their garden of 1850. Later, pumps driven by wind power, raised the water from the tules for irrigation, while later, water was taken raw from the river for all purposes. In 1867, W. W. Smith built a water wheel for the purpose of obtaining water for his ranch purposes and to have power for running a grist mill, turning the grindstone and other mechanical needs. At one time, water was so scarce in Antioch that it sold in 5-gallon cans for home use.

Until 1920, a great part of the Diablo Valley near the mountain was devoted to dry farming of wheat and barley and stock raising. It was only on the lower elevations that farming to any large extent was profitable. Under the influence of irrigation, the land progressed rapidly. In 1925, there were 42,000 acres under the irrigation. The Brentwood, Knightsen and Lone Tree Irrigation districts cooperatively own the East Contra Costa Irrigation Company and main distributing ditch from which they obtain water pumped from Indian Slough.

By a series of booster pumps the water is elevated to a height of 140 feet at its furthest point from the river in the Lone Tree District. Numerous laterals tap the main ditch; and by this means and the aid of concrete pipe lines, the land is thoroughly watered.

In the Oakley Section west to Antioch, Irrigation is carried on from individual wells. These wells are from 150 feet to 250 feet deep. Little difficulty has been experienced in striking a plentiful water supply.

Those who knew of Dr. Marsh's prophesy, "of a rich, fertile valley extending from his home to the river, irrigated from the waters of Marsh Creek. Those who settled on that land since 1865, have seen the change from dry farming to alfalfa fields, orchards, vineyards, and truck gardens over the 13,316 acres formerly owned by Dr. Marsh. The average orchard in 1925 was 20 to 40 acres.

View of Kimball Island north of Antioch. Taken in 1971 from G and First streets.

Southeastern Antioch from Hill 13. Almond orchard in bloom can be seen center and right. Photo taken in 1971.

Antioch to the northwest from Hill 13. Mount Helene is left center. Photo taken in 1971.

In the early 1860s, encroachment of salt water into fresh water areas of the lower Sacramento and San Joaquin River brought about the idea of the building of a dam to prevent salt water infiltration of the Delta and rich lands of the river. The dam was to be built below the confluence of the two rivers. In 1873, 1879–80, the dam was again considered. The idea strung along for many years. More and more fresh water was being drawn because of the growth of the farming area. The final solution was the inclusion of the Contra Costa Canal in the massive Central Valley Project.

Antioch pier at A Street, original location of Distillery wharf. Used today by Hickmott.

Part IV Farming, Produce and Climate 99

Two plaques at the foot of F Street. Birthplace of Antioch. Rails that were laid from the coal mines down F Street to the coal wharf. Photo taken in 1970.

"The pioneer days of Antioch are part of a past century. There are both good and evil in them, as there are in these days. Let the evils be forgotten except to remember with thankfulness that they are past, as time, like our ever-flowing river bears us onward at last to the ocean of peace," said Louisa A. Schott in her speech to the Woman's Club of Antioch, September 1929.

Antioch is a happy place, a busy place, a bit over-organized perhaps, but we are proud of our accomplishments, our beautiful location, our standing as a residential city, our industrial and agricultural importance, our nearness to all the advantages of the "Big Cities", and our nearness to all the sport areas of river and mountains. Antioch's roots are deep and finely planted in the embryonic stage of the western "Yankee America".

Miss Ada Culver's Millinery Store.

Dunnigan's Drug Store.

Hotel Brentwood.

The Second Hotel Brentwood built 1911 by Balfour Guthrie & Co., San Francisco.

BIBLIOGRAPHY

History of Contra Costa County (1882, 1917, 1926)

C.C.C. Historical Society, Illustrations of Contra Costa County, California

Smith C., Diary of W. W. Smith

Schott J. and A., Diaries and Articles of John and Louisa A. Schott

Braun L. T., Mineral Commodities of California, Bulletin No. 56 (State Division of Mines, 1950)

Various, (Antioch Ledger 1870 to 1835, 1964–65)

Bridge Opening Supplement, (Antioch Ledger January 1926)

The Golden Link, (Antioch Ledger June 1924)

Antioch Centennial Ledger (July 5, 1951)

Pennington, Wm. A., Oakland Tribune Knave (November 18, 1945)

H. J. Corcoran, Various Articles (Stockton Record 1919)

M. Hust, Antioch High School

G. M. Kimball, Books, Maps and Store Ledger

Board of Trustees and City Council Minutes (1872)

Contra Costa County Office of the Superintendent of Schools

Beede, Mr. and Mrs. R., Experiences and pictures from

Turner, Mrs. J., Experiences and pictures from

Showers, Mrs. I., Experiences and pictures from

Schott, F. T., Experiences and pictures from

Flaherty, A., Experiences, Articles and pictures from

McKellips, D. O., Articles and pictures from

Dunton, P., Articles and pictures from

Ginochio Family, L., Pictures from

Meeker, Mrs., Pictures from

Uren, T. H. Material furnished by

Wrinkle, Mrs. S, Article from

Bibliography

Williams, Mrs. L, Article from

Draper, R., Information from

Booth, M., Sketches by

Rozie's Portraits, Restored pictures by

The Antioch Bridge shortly after opening in January 1926. Note the car ferry from Sherman Island is still carrying traffic. It is approaching the Antioch mole/terminus.

SELECTED READING

Antioch Chamber of Commerce, *About Antioch, California* (Antioch: Chamber of Commerce, 1958)

Antioch Historical Society, Bohakel, C. et al., *Images of America, Antioch* (San Francisco: Arcadia Publishing, 2005)

Antioch Ledger, "Progress Development Edition: Illustrated Folio Magazine" (Antioch: *The Antioch Ledger*, 1948)

Bohakel, C., Gorospe, L., Bruton, T., Norway, J., *A Walker's Guide to Old Town Antioch* (Antioch: privately published 1983, revised edition 1989)

California State Chamber of Commerce, Industrial Plan Location Committee, *Standard Industrial Survey Summary Report, Antioch* (Sacramento: State Chamber of Commerce, 1958)

Cook, F. (ed.), *Antioch Centennial Almanac* (Volcano: California Traveler, 1972)

Freemasons, Antioch Lodge No. 175, *Centennial 1865-1965* (Pittsburg: Miller Print, 1965)

Historical Record Company, *History of Contra Costa County, California with Biographic Sketches* (Los Angeles: Historical Record Company, 1926)

Hohlmayer, E., *Looking Back II: Tales of Old East Contra Costa County* (Antioch: E. and N. Hohlmayer, 1996)

Hohlmayer, E., *Looking Back: Tales of Old Antioch and Other Places* (Visalia: Jostens Printing and Publishing Division, 1991)

Hulaniski, F. J.(ed.), *The History of Contra Costa County* (Berkeley: The Elms Publishing Company, Inc., 1917)

Kishaba, R. *The History of Nortonville* (Held by the Antioch Public Library, unpublished manuscript, 1961)

Lew, E., *The House of Liu: A Han Dynasty Genealogy, A 5,000-year Heritage, the Journey to America* (Lathrop, CA: The Lew Press, 2012)

Lopez, F., *A History of Antioch, California* (Held by the Antioch Public Library, unpublished manuscript, 1972)

Lyman, G., *John Marsh, Pioneer: The Life Story of a Trail-Blazer on Six Frontiers* (San Franciso: Byron Hot Springs, originally published 1930, Reprinted 2012)

Marks, D., *Historical Summarization of the City of Antioch: Incorporated February 6, 1872* (Antioch: City Clerk's Office, 1985)

Metcalfe, W., *Souvenir Contra Costa Conty California as Reviewed Under the Vitascope: A Pen Picture of its Wonderful Productive Valleys Superbly Illustrated* (Richmond: The Richmond Record, 1902)

Munro-Fraser, J.P., *The History of Contra Costa County* (San Francisco: Slocum & Co.,1882)

Parent, T., *Rose Hill: A Comprehensive History of a Pioneer Cemetery in the Mount Diablo Coal Field, Contra Costa County, California* (Oakland: East Bay Regional Park District, 2011)

Purcell, M., *The History of Contra Costa County* (Berkeley: Gillick Press, 1940)

Reynolds, F., *Antioch-Sherman Island Bridge: Specifications for Constructing a Steel and Reinforced Concrete Bridge Across the San Joaquin River About Three Miles East of Antioch, California for the American Toll Bridge Company and Delta Bridge Corporation* (San Francisco: J.G. Little & Co., 1924)

Schott, A., *Antioch School in Pioneer Days* (Amongst papers held by Lennie Marshy Wolfe, unpublished manuscript, undated)

Schott, L., *The Early Days of Antioch* (Held by the Antioch Public Library, unpublished manuscript, undated)

Smith and Elliot, *Illustrations of Contra Costa County, California* (Sacramento: Smith and Elliot, 1952)

Tatam, R., *Old Times in Contra Costa: A Journey to the Past* (Pittsburg: Highland Publishers, 1993)

Tornhelm, W., Hust M., Cox L. (ed.), *Antioch Schools, Contra Costa County* (Pleasant Hill: Public Library, 1970)

U. S. Department of Commerce, *San Francisco Bay to Antioch California Small-Craft Chart: Coast and Geodetic Survey* (Washington DC: U. S. Department of Commerce, 1961)

INDEX

A

Abbott, Elvina G., 71
Abbott, J. F., 22
Abbott, J. P., 19, 20, 26, 27, 52, 69, 71, 77, 81
Abbott, Millie G., 71
Abbott, Stephen, 20
Abbott, Warren, 20, 58
Abella, Ramon, 3
Abrams, Will, 58
Adams, Dr., 7
Adams, Norman, 69
Adler, Aaron, 41
advertisements, 43–44, 47, 49
agriculture, 85–99. *See also individual crops*
Albion Pottery, 40
alfalfa, 88, 94–95, 97
almonds, 87, 88, 89, 96, 98
American Toll Bridge Company, 52, 54
Ancient Order of United Workers, 69
Antioch
    birthplace of, 99
    Board of Trustees of, 20, 22
    boundaries of, 20
    climate of, 85, 91
    elevation of, 91–92
    incorporation of, 19–20
    location of, 91
    map (1900), xiv–xvii
    naming of, 6
    ordinances of, 20–22, 27
    other towns named, in U.S., 7
    population of, in 1890, 23
    previous names of, 3, 5
    street names of, 23, 27
    surveys of, 12
Antioch Bank of Savings, 50
Antioch Board of Trade, 69
Antioch Bridge, 52–54
Antioch Chamber of Commerce, 69
Antioch City Hall, 17, 18, 44, 54
Antioch Distillery Co., 17, 40–41
Antioch District High School, 64–65
Antioch Drug Store, 49
Antioch Glass and Mirror Company, 38
Antioch Grammar School, 56, 57, 59, 61, 65, 67, 72
Antioch Grange, 17, 38
Antioch Hardware and Furniture Company, 48, 49
Antioch Hotel, 23, 44, 73
Antioch Ice and Fuel Co., 43, 44
Antioch-Live Oak Unified School District, 65
Antioch Lumber Company, 9, 17, 38–40, 49
Antioch Paper Mill, 45
Antioch Planing Mill, 68
Antioch Union High School, 60, 61
Antioch Woman's Club, 71, 72, 78, 99
apricots, 88, 94, 95
Arata, Eugene, 27
Arata, Frank S., 86
Arata, J., 50
Arata Building, 23, 73
Arata family, 86
Arata Grocery, 78
Arlington Hotel, 23, 25, 29, 48, 49, 50, 53, 75
asparagus, 12–13, 88, 93–94
Avery, H. R., 58
Azevedo, Manuel, 51
Azevedo home, 83

B

Babbe Landing, 85
Baker, Alda, 65
Baker, Alice E., 71
Baker, Henry N., 19
Baker, H. W., 68, 69
Baker, Ina, 48
Baker, J. Rio, 8, 22, 48, 49, 50, 52, 68, 69, 70, 83
Baker and George Drug Store, 23, 46
Baker Hardware, 46
Baler, Mrs., 70
Banchero, Sarah, 58
band, 55
The Band of Hope, 66
Bank of America, 25, 50
Bank of Antioch, 49
banks, 49–50
Barker, Mr., 31

barley, 92, 93, 95, 97
Barnett, C. T., 51
Barnhurst, John, 73
Barron, Joseph P., 20
Barrows, D. D., 69
Bassett, Charles, 62
Baules, Joseph, 20
beans, 88, 92, 94
Beata, M., 50
Beede, Abbott and Simpson Lumber Co., 38, 39
Beede, Albert T., 69
Beede, Anna, 71
Beede, Helen, 63
Beede, Henry F., 38, 39, 46, 61, 69, 70, 92
Beede, H. H., 49
Beede, Margaret E., 70, 71
Beede, Nell, 71
Beede, Ralph, 38, 39, 40, 51, 67, 83
Beede home, 91, 92
Beemer, Mr., 2
beets, 88, 92, 94
Belshaw, Charles, 37
Belshaw, C. M., 26, 71, 72, 79
Belshaw, Mrs. C. M., 70, 72
Belshaw, C. W., 69
Belshaw, Jay, 20, 70
Belshaw, John, 20
Belshaw, J. T., 24, 26, 35, 36, 70, 81
Belshaw, M. W., 32, 34, 36, 40, 83
Belshaw, T. J., 59
Belshaw, W. W., 24
Belshaw and Company, 33
Belshaw home, 24, 75, 79, 81, 83
Belshaw Store and Theater, 20, 68
Benson, Andy, 88
Benyo, Mike and Catherine, 83
Biglow, Carlton, 60, 61
Biglow, Cellus, 71
Biglow, Frank, 48, 71
Biglow, Judson, 62, 66
Biglow, Parlman, 88
Biglow and Joslin, 49
Biglow Ranch, 40
Black Diamond claim, 32, 36
Blackledge, Reverend James, 68
Blanchard, Kemer, 16
boat travel, 46
Bollinger, J. E., 20
Bonnickson, Jack, 86
Boobar, Drusella, 66
Boobar, James, 12, 15, 17, 34, 38
Boothby, Mr., 29
Bower, Marion, 63
Bowers Rubber Works, 54

Brewer, H. W., 20
Breyer, H. J., 69
bricks, 31
bridges, 52–54
Brill, Dr., 68
Brink, Albert, 20
Broad, Nels, 88
Brown, A., 20
Brown, Collins, 77
Brown, E. E., 26
Brown, George W., 20, 22, 66
Brown, Peter and James, 45
Brown and Baker Hardware Store, 48, 49, 77
Brown and George Farm Machinery, 47
Brown home, 83
Brun family, 87
Brunkhorst, W. A., 19
buckwheat, 92
Buffo, Joe, 58
Buffo, John, 58
Buffo, Lorenzo, 58
Bullock, Charles, 67
Bullock, William, 36
Bullock home, 24, 35, 75
Bummers Corner, 77
Burton, Noah, 68
Byron Hot Springs, iv, 103

C

cabbage, 94
California Distilling Company, 41, 44
California Packet, 5
California Paper and Board Mill, 45
Callaghan, Father Patrick, 67
Campbell, Mary, 70
Canssi, John, 88
Caple, Jack, 66
Carey, James, 71
Carman, G. S., 20
Carman and Israel Grocery, 42, 43
Carman home, 4, 81
Carnegie Fund, 72
Carolan, James, 71
The Caroline, 54
Carpenter, Dr., 68
Carpenter, Miss, 58
Carter, T. O., 15, 20
Casino Theater, 38, 40, 51, 54
Cater, Mr., 64
cattle, 96–97
celery, 88, 94
cemeteries, 15, 16, 78
Central mine, 32, 33, 36
Central Pacific Railroad, 90

Central Valley Project, 26, 98
Cervans, Joe, 49
Chane Stables, 29
Charnock, Richard, 69
Chase & Robbins Livery Stable, 18, 43, 44
Cheney, Cyrus, 19
cherries, 94
Chinatown, 19
Chittenden, J. A., 20
Christian Advent Church, 68
churches, 65–69
City Market, 44
City Wharf, 17
Clark, Mrs. M. J., 68
Cleaver, D., 18, 69
Cleaves, D. N., 20
climate, 85, 91
coal mining, 28, 31–37
Comers, Francis, 32
Congregational Church, 8, 56, 66–67, 68, 78
Conroy, James, 20
Contra Costa Canal, 25, 98
Contra Costa County, naming of, 26
Cooley, Mr., 42
Cooney, Al, 51, 65, 67
Cooney, Francis, 62, 65, 66, 67
Cooney home, 24, 35, 75, 80
copper, 37–38
corn, 92, 93, 94, 95
Cossan, J. T., 19
Cox, John Thomas, 82
Cramer, Don, 65
Crawford, Elmer, 66
Creary, George J., 65
Crespi, Father, 3
Cronan, Ramona, 70
Cruickshank, James, 58
Cruiksbank, James, 32
Cryon, Thomas, 69
cucumbers, 94
Culver, Ada, 99
Cushing, James T., 20, 23

D

Dahnken, Fred, 52
Dahnken, Henry, 71
Dahnken, Louis, 36, 69
Darby, A. G., 89
Davidson family, 86
Davis, Pearl, 58
Davis, Roy V., 52
Dearien, H. H., 20
Dearien, William H., 24, 34
Deithelm family, 87

Delta Bridge Corporation, 52
Delta region, 85, 88–89, 93–95
Dennison, Mr., 4
DeWitt home, 82
Diablo, Mt., 3, 8, 28, 32, 33, 37, 65, 96
Diablo Valley, 7, 85, 87, 94–97
Dickinson, Charles, 62
Dickinson Hotel, 48, 49
dikes, 17
Distillery Wharf, 39, 51, 98
distilling, 40–41
Dixon, Miss, 58
Dodge, George A., 24
Dohyns, William H., 69
Donlon, James, 44, 67
Donlon, M., 19
Donlon, Peter, 20, 44, 51, 67
Donlon Drayage, 43, 44
Donlon home, 42, 80
Donlon Ice and Fuel, 75
Douglass, C. B., 96
Douglass, Martha, 6
Douglass, Robert, 4, 5
Doulan, John, 20
Downing, Arvilla McMullen, 62
Dunnigan home, 8, 22
Dunnigan's Drug Store, 99
Dunton, Adelbert, 62

E

Earl, Mr., 73
earthquakes, 31, 33, 67, 71–72
Easley, Robert P., 26
Eddy, B., 69
Eddy, Russell, 12, 15, 26, 43
Eddy Survey, 12
Edward, Bennie, 58
eggplant, 94
El Campanil Theater, 50, 51, 59
Elmore, Margaret, 61
Empire mine, 32–37
Empire Railroad, 35, 36
Enterprise, 9
Eureka Market, 47
Evans, Ellis, 67
Evans, Minta, 71
Ewing, James, 19, 20
Express, 47

F

Fages, Don Pedro, 3
Famous Fashion Store, 4, 48
Farland, H. L., 20
farming, 85–99. *See also individual crops*

108   Index

Fassett, H. W., 20
ferries, 47, 52, 54, 85
Field brothers, 83
figs, 95
fire department, 23–24, 54
fires, 18
First National Bank of Antioch, 50
Fisher, P. M., 59
Fitzpatrick, Jim, 86
Fitzpatrick, John, 86
Flackhammer family, 87
Flaherty, A., 19, 65
Forest, 1
Forman, Billy, 77
Forman, Katie E., 71
Forman, William F., 89
Forman, William R., 7, 8, 48
Forman home, 37
Foster, Granville P., 60, 61
Foster, H. A., 20
Fourth of July celebrations, 23, 25, 55
Fowler, Bishop H. L., 68
Fraga, Joe, 88
Francis, 85
fraternal organizations, 69, 71
Free Masons and Odd Fellow Cemetery, 15, 16, 78
Frink, C. H., 71
Frink, Mary E., 71
Fuller, E. G., 19
Fuller, E. J., 20
Fuller, Madam, 7
Fuller, Robert, 7, 89
Fuller, R. R., 20
Fuller home, 9
Fulton, Mary, 72
Fulton Shipyard, 40, 47, 76, 85

G

Gagen, John, 42
Gain, Tom, 7
Gaines, Thomas, 44, 52, 66
Galloway, Joseph, 12, 17, 19, 24, 38, 66
Galloway, Mrs. Joseph, 66
Galloway home, 81
garbage dump, 27
Gard, James, 20
Gardner, H., 19
George, Alice V., 71
George, Frank, 27, 68
George, Mrs. Frank, 27
George, Lola, 71
George, Dr. Worth Scott, 17, 27, 50, 69, 70, 73
George, Mrs. W. S., 27, 70
Gilchrist, William, 7

Ginnocchio, Amelia, 58
Ginnocchio, Louis, 58
Ginocchio family, 86
Girvan, William, 69
Glass, Stonewall, 66
Glenn, Miss, 62
God's Acres, 16
Good Templars Lodge, 71, 72
Grange associations, 17, 38
grapes, 88, 94, 95–96
Graves, Amos M., 89
Gridley, Orville, 61
Griffin, P., 20
Griffin, Thomas, 71
Griffin, Willie, 51
Griffin Hotel, 18
Griswold, Carrie, 13, 16
Griswold, Mr., 16
Gruenwald, George, 20, 41
guavas, 93

H

Hagmeyer, Emelie, 63
Hagmire, Emily, 62
Hagstrom, Helen E., xix
Hale, Bob, 8
Hammond, W. W., 96
Hanford, Avery, 52
Hard, R. B., 20, 22, 26, 31
Hard, Rozwell, 69
Harding, J. L., 50
Harding, Juliette C., 71
Hardy, Charles S., 71
Harkinson, H. F., 49
Harkinson, Mazie, 70
Harkinson, Mrs., 70, 71
Harkinson, R., 69, 70, 77
Harkinson home, 82
Harris, Peter, 87
Hartley, A. C., 59
Hartley, Annie J., 71
Hartley Building, 42
Hartley mine, 36
Haven, Mr., 58
Hawxhurst, George W., 32, 33, 35, 48
Hawxhurst, Josie, 65
Hawxhurst home, 82
hay, 88, 92, 94
Hayes home, 80
Heath home, 83
Heinoch, T. Aug., 20
Helene, Mount, 98
Henderson, James, 7, 9
Henderson, Jane, 9

Hespian, 45
Hickmott, R., 90
Hickmott Canning Company, 78, 94
Higgins, Helen Stokes, 62, 63
Hillegas, William, 32
Hiram Hills farm, 90
Hobson, Emma, 60, 61
Hoey, Valona, 71
Hoffman, Ferdinand and Christian, 7
Hoffman, Judge, 10
hogs, 96, 97
Hoien, Jim "Clock," 50
Hollender building, 31
Holy Rosary Church, 31, 63, 68
Homberg Hall, 68
Homburg, M., 20
Home Bakery, 74
Hooper, C. A., 63
Hopkins, Dick, 74
Hop Lee's wash house, 18–19
Hoppe, M. C., 71
Hornback home, 24
horses, 97
Hotel Brentwood, 100
House, G., 71
House Barber Shop, 23
House Hardware, 48
Houston, R. G., 20
Howard, Dr. J. P., 18
Howard, J. R., 20
Humble, Christian, 20
Huntery Livery, 51, 53
Hurst, Miss, 67
Hust, Mabelle, 64
Hustels, Mr., 7

I
Indigenous people, 2–3
International Order of Odd Fellows, 69
Iron House Landing, 85
irrigation, 89, 97
Irvine, Edna Peters, 62, 63
Irwin, Margaret, 62
Isreal, Mr., 32

J
Jack Wolfe Hardware Store, 42
Jacobs, M. H., 20, 47
Jacobs, Mrs. T. B., 71
Jarvis Brothers Shipyard, 47
Jensen, Carol A., vii
Jensen, Hans, 86
Jessie, Fred, 88
Jessup, Alyszan R., 71
Jessup, Oscar M., 20
Jessup, S., 43
Jessup, Stephen, 20, 23, 69
Joe Ross Store, 42, 44, 47, 53, 75
John Muir School, 59
Johnson, William C., 19
Jones, John, 62
Jones, J. W., 23
Jones, William, 19
Joralomon, Eugene, 61
Josleu, S., 23
Joslin, Arba, 60, 61
Joslin, Miss, 71
Joslin, S. B., 10, 20
Joslin Harness Shop, 26
Jost and Adler, 41
Jost Distillery, 41
Judson, A., 86
Judson, E., 32, 34
Judson, Pharcellus K., 86
Judsonville, 32, 35
Juett, Bedson, 62, 66

K
Keeney, Mrs. C. W., 72
Keeney, Fannie Mason, 72
Keeney, Fannie N., 71
Keeney, H. D., 45
Keeney, M. D., 44
Keeney, Will, 45
Keeney home, 75, 82
Kelley, Loretta, 62
Kelley, Nellie Beede, 62, 63
Kelley Funeral Home, 49
Kenney, Emerson and Collins, 45
Kerns, John, 86
Killicum, John S., 69
kilns, 31
Kimball, Adelia Barrett (Mrs. John Schott), 6, 9, 14, 56, 57, 66
Kimball, Caroline Barrett, 15
Kimball, Carrie. *See* Griswold, Carrie
Kimball, Edgar H., 6, 11, 14
Kimball, Captain George W., i, 3–5, 7, 9–17, 20, 65, 66, 67, 90
Kimball, Sadie. *See* Wrinkle, Sadie
Kimball, S. P., 4, 7
Kimball and Co., 12
Kimball General Store, 14
Kimball home, 5, 24, 49, 57, 73, 75, 81, 90
Kimball Island, 4, 10, 11, 13, 90
Kirker Creek, 3
Kirker Pass, 7, 9
Kittredge, H., 63

Klatt, Oscar H., 52
Klengel, Mr., 5
Klengel, Otto E., 47
Knapp, Mr., 18
Knight, William, 40
Kohn, Charles, 19
kumquats, 93

L

Laird, William, 62
Lancaster, 15
land grants, 1, 10–12
Lauritzen, Andrew, 72
Lauritzen, Chris, 52
Lauritzen, F. C., 52
Lauritzen Transportation Company, 52
Lawrence, Johnny, 88
Leam, Robert, 36
Ledger, 19, 27, 43–44, 45, 49, 61
LeQuenel, Madame, 43
lettuce, 94
levees, 88
Levy, M. S., 19, 20, 23, 69
Levy Wharf, 16
Lewis, J. H., 20
Lewis, W. C., 62
libraries, 72–73
Little, S. G., 49
L. Meyers Store, 25, 46, 50
Lobree, I., 20, 40
Lock, W., 9
Lone Tree Way, 86
Long, William, 23
loquats, 93
Lougbef, Alice, 58
Louise, Alice, 71
Low, Abraham, 20
Ludinghouse and Son, 47, 49
lumber, 38–40
Lumber Wharf, 32
Lynch, Willie Williamson, 62
Lynn, Emma Bolz, 65, 70

M

Mahan, D. P., 20
maps
    Antioch (1900), xiv–xvii
    area (1880), xi–xiii
    coal mines and railroads of Mt. Diablo, 28
Marble, A. M., 20
Marchetti home, 24
Markowitz, A. J., 50
Marquetti's, 21
Marsh, Charles, 9, 15, 81
Marsh, Dr. John, 2, 9, 10, 33, 86, 96, 97
Marshall, Benjamin, 4, 6
Marsh grant, 10, 12
Marsh Landing, 7, 50, 73, 85
Martin, James, 19
Martin, Thomas, 20
Martinoni, Elmer, 67
Mason home, 82, 83
Masonic Hall, 40
Mayon, D., 20
McCartney, D., 20, 47
McCartney home, 18
McCarty, J. D., 44
McCoy, George, 20
McCoy's shop, 18
McDaniel, F., 19
McDermott, P., 20
McFarlane, Frank, 20
McFarlon, Frank, 86
McGrath home, 75
McKellips, Annie F., 71
McKellips, Annie T., 71
McKellips, Dan, 70
McKellips, D. O., 36
McKellips, S. H., 34, 35, 36, 37
McKellips home, 8, 81
McKinley, William, 71
McMalon, T. A., 12
McMaster, J. C., 1, 7, 9, 15, 19, 20, 26, 31, 44
McNulty, J. J., 20, 69
McQuade ranch, 86
McVeigh, Nick, 36
Los Medaños Grant, 1, 10, 11, 12
Meek, Bill, 93
Meeker, Mr., 68
melons, 94
Mesa, José Antonio, 1, 2
Methodist Church, 63, 68–69
Meyer, G., 83
Meyer, L., 56, 69
Meyer, Mrs. L., 70
Meyer, Mildred A., 71
Meyer, Sophie, 70, 71
Milan, Tom, 96
Millard, Ruth, 63
Miller, Captain, 9
Miller, George, 20
Miller, J., 24
Mills, E. T., 69
Mitchel, Maria, 6
Mitchell, Captain, 5–6
Mitchell, Miss, 58
Montgomery, Archbishop, 67
Montgomery, C. F., 71, 72

Montgomery, Charles F., 19, 59, 70, 77
Montgomery, Curtis F., 19, 70
Montgomery, D. F., 69
Montgomery, Mrs., 71, 72
Moore, Dr. and Mrs., 70, 71
Moore, Walter, 62
Moore, W. C., 62
Moore, W. S., 61
Morgan, Reverend C., 66
Morrisey, M. A., 19
Morrisey's Corner, 49
Morrison, Annie (Mrs. Joseph Galloway), 66
Muir School, 6
mulberry trees, 85, 90
Mulhare, John, 67
Mulhare, Joseph, 71
Municipal Wharf, 16
Musselman, Gilbert, 89

N
National Trust and Savings Bank, 50
Native Sons of the Golden West, 71
nectarines, 93
Newbert, Herman G., 50
Newman, William, 7
New York House, 2, 3
New York of the Pacific, 1–2, 15
New York Township, 5
Nicholson, I., 40
Nicholson, J., 20
Noia, Robert, 88
Norton, Noah, 32
Nortonville, 32, 34

O
Oak Springs ranch, 86
oats, 92, 93
O'Brien, Carl, 94
O'Brien, John C., 6, 7, 12, 69, 89
O'Brien Hall, 23, 26
O'Hara, Jim, 87
olives, 95
Olsen, Araminta Evans, 62
Ong, Jackson W., 69
onions, 88, 92, 94
Order of the Eastern Star, 71
ordinances, early, 20–22
Osgood, Mr., 34
Ott, Joseph, 19, 43

P
Page, Elmer, 36
Page, S. G., 44
Page, S. T., 20

Palace Hotel, 23, 49
paper milling, 44–45
Paraffine Paint Company, 45
Parker, William, 1
Parkison, Alice, 71
Parkison, R. H., 71
Peabody's, 86
peaches, 88, 89, 94, 95
peanuts, 85
pears, 88, 93, 94
peas, 92
Peers, Charles, 19
Peoche, Manuel, 11
peppers, 94
Perry, George, 20
persimmons, 93
Peters, Fred, 65
Peterson, D. J., 14
Peterson, Nelson, 47, 48, 80
petroleum, 38
Petrovich, Nick, 51
Phalin, Superintendent, 61
Phelps, R. S., 64
Phillips, Van W., 19, 24
Pioneer Soda Works, 42
Pitts, Mrs., 70
Pitts, S. Franklin, 19
Pitts, S. S., 20
Pittsburg High School, 64
Pitts home, 82
plums, 88
"The Point," 3, 17, 29, 51
pomegranates, 93
Portman, Andrew, 7
post offices, 15, 46
potatoes, 92, 94
pottery, 40
poultry raising, 96
Preston, J. C., 90
Prewett, J. C., 50
prices, 14
Prohibition, 27
prunes, 88
Psyche family, 16
Pulsifer, Deacon John, 3, 6
Pulsifer, Joseph, 3
Pulsifer Brothers, 97
Purchase, Will, 20

R
Rafitt, Frank, 88
railroads, 15, 28, 33–37, 46
Rapp, Ed, 20
Rattan, Dr. Frank, 69, 83

recipes, 74, 76–77
Records, Frank, 89
Redding, Cassie, 62
Red Front Bar, 11
Reed, H. B., 20, 47
Reed, Putnam, 36
Remfree, V., 44
Remfree home, 80
Rhamm, John, 87
rhubarb, 94
Rialto, 1
Rietoro, H., 20
Riley, Father Alphonsus, 67
Ring, Ana, 65
Rivera, Captain, 3
River Express Co., 47
Riverview Union High School, 61–64
Robins, G. B., 19
Robinson, Frank, 71
Robinson, L. L., 11
Rodgers, Jack, 11, 29, 41
Rodgers, M. S., 11
Rogers, Dr., 68
Rogers building, 31
Rose, Joe, 88
Ross, Joe, 42, 44, 47
Roundtree, Mr., 86
Rountree, W., 19
Rouse, Beede and Abbott Lumber Co., 38, 49
Rouse, Dave, 37
Rouse, Mrs. J., 70
Rouse, J. C., 32, 33, 49, 69, 70
Rouse home, 81
Ruckstuhl family, 87
Russell, George, 40
rye, 92, 95

S

Sacramento River, 3, 25–26, 37, 39, 91, 98
Sanchez, José Antonio, 3
San Joaquin Apartments, 73
San Joaquin River, 1, 3, 19, 20, 25, 37, 39, 52, 91, 98
San Pablo and Tulare Railroad, 15, 46
Santa Fe Depot, xx, 27
Santa Fe Railroad, 37, 40, 41, 46, 50, 64
Sater, Leila, 65
Scauton, Edna, 58
schools, viii, 56, 57–65
Schott, Mrs. A. B. *See* Kimball, Adelia Barrett (Mrs. John Schott)
Schott, Franklin T., 60, 61
Schott, George, 56, 57
Schott, John, 6, 12, 57
Schott, Louisa A., 99

Schott home, 54, 56, 75
Schultz, Martha, 63
Scouts Hall, 72, 73, 75
Seers, H., 20
Sellers, Mr. and Mrs., 90
Sellers, William, 17
Shattuck, T. K., 32
sheep, 96–97
Sheirwelup, Joseph, 20
Sherman Island, 10, 13, 86, 89
Shine, T. P., 51
Showers, Imogene Belshaw, 62
Shreve, Ada, 63
silkworms, 85, 90
Simpson, Captain A. H., 38
Smith, Benjamin, 15
Smith, C. H., 19
Smith, Charles, 71
Smith, Charles L., 3, 11, 15
Smith, Charles V., 7
Smith, Frank, 86
Smith, James F., 15
Smith, Reverend Joseph Horton, 1–3, 6
Smith, Joseph L., 3, 11, 15, 20
Smith, Mary E., 71
Smith, May Cooney, 62
Smith, N. W., 71
Smith, Roy, 62
Smith, Sarah, 3, 6, 15
Smith, William M., 15
Smith, Reverend William Wiggin, 1–6, 9–11, 15, 16, 24, 29, 31, 67, 97
Smith's Landing, 4
Smith's Point, 3, 85
soil types, 87–88
Somerhalder, G., 96
Somers, Francis, 32, 33
Somersville, 32, 33
Sorgenfrey, Alice, 58
Southern Pacific Railroad, 15, 29, 46, 50
squash, 94
Stain, Ferdinand, 19
Stamm, Ferd, 40, 51, 67, 82
Stamm Brothers, 47
Stevenson, J. D., 1
Stewart, W. B., 32
Stewartsville, 32
Stichfield, Herbert, 15
Stinchfield, Annie, 58, 59
Stinchfield, Paul, 65
strawberries, 95
street names, 23, 27
Strickfield, P., 20
Strickler, John W., 20

Sullenger, Bill, 88
Sutton, Thomas, 23
Swain, Mrs. Fred, 70
Swain, George A., 20
Swain, Mr., 65
Sweeney, Charles, 23, 51, 71
Sweeney, Ed, 66
sweet potatoes, 92

T

Tappeinen, John, 20
Tapperner's Shoe Store, 18
Taylor, R., 20
telephones, 46
Tellus, Tony, 66
theaters, 50, 51
Thompson, Mr., 7
Thurber, A., 58
Thyarks, George, 20, 69
Thyarks home, 82
timeline, xviii
Timms Millinery, 49
tomatoes, 88, 94
Tope, John, 71
Tormey, Tom, 86
Townsend, J. E., 19
train depot, xx
Tregallus, Mr., 15
Trembath, R. J., 26
Trembath and Frederickson, 48, 49
Treugrove, Mr., 23
Tron House, 9
Trythall, Helen, 62
Tuck, Abigail, 9
tule, 2, 41–42
Turner, Ben, 48
Turner, Jean Baker, 48, 70, 83
Turner, John B., 20
Turner Brothers, 50
Tuttle, Jay, 20
Tyler Hotel, 21

U

Union Hall, 29, 69
Union Hotel, 43
Union mine, 32
Upham, George, 12
Uren, Richard, 71
Uren, T. H., 86
Uren, Tom, 46, 86
Utter, William, 66

V

Vallejo, M. G., 3

Vanderbundt Brothers, 96
Van Voorbis, Ruel, 66
Veale, R. R., 26
Veale, R. R., Jr., 71
Viera, Cyril, 62
Viera, Joe G., 89
Viera, John F., 88, 89
Viera, Manuel, 86, 88
Vimpez, Father Vincent, 67
Vollmer, Frederick, 19

W

Waite, Harry, 19
Waldie, Arch, 51
Waldie, Jerome, 80
Waldie home, 80
Wall, Ethel, 65
Wall, Robert, 23
Wall, Roscoe, 62, 67
Wallace, Tom, 86
Wall Shoe Store, 23, 25
Wally, R. J., 20
walnuts, 88, 96
Walton, J. P., 69
Ward, Edna Schultz, 62
Ward law offices, 19
Warren, J. H., 66
Warren, Job E., 20
water, 24–26, 97–98. *See also* irrigation
Weaver, H. A., 19
Wehie, Frank, 89
Wein, Charles, 20
Welch, Tip, 88
Weldie home, 8
Wemple, Dr., 8, 83
Wemple, E. L., 69
Wenig, H. C., 69
West, Mrs. H. A., 72
West, Herbert A., 50
West, J. A., 50
West, Robert, 19
West Harley mine, 36
wharves, 16–17, 50
wheat, 9, 44, 90, 92, 93, 95, 97
Wheelehen, Eugene, 71
Wheelehen, John, 71
Whelihan, Mr. and Mrs. John, 86
Whipple, S. B., 32
Whitfield, Dr. and Mrs. Albert, 70
Whitfield, Bud, 71
Whitfield, Frances, 71
Whitfield, Jackson, 71
Whitfield, John, 71
Whitfield, Lily, 71

Whitfield, Ramona, 71
Wilbur, I. R., 86
Wildening, F., 69
Wilkening, Fred, 19, 23
Wilkening home, 82
William Island, 90
Williams, Elizabeth, 71
Williams, F., 23
Williams, Francis, 20, 69
Williams, George M., 73
Williams, Reverend James, 69
Williams, Maggie, 56, 57
Williams, Miss, 58
Williams, Mrs., 72
Williamson, H., 20
Williamson, W. C., 50
Willow Pass, 3
Wills, Dr. C. A., 70
Wills, F. M., 71
Wills, Frank, 20, 23, 51, 60, 61, 70
Wills, Josiah, 90
Wills, Mrs. T., 17
Wills, T. M., 89
Wills, T. N., 20, 22, 81
Will's farmhouse, 8, 12
Wills Ranch, 11
Wilson, C. M., 37
Winter Island, 13
Wolcott, Fred, 51
Wolcott, Oliver, 19
Wolf, Kahn and Co., 44
Wolf and Company, 12
Woodruff, David, 66
Woodruff, Mrs., 58
Woolan, Jennie Bullock, 62, 63
Worrell, E. C., 50
Worrell home, 22, 80
Wright, G. E., 20
Wright, John E., 69
Wrinkle, Sadie, 13, 16
Wyatt, Mr., 7, 12

X
Xavier, Tony, 88

Y
Yoast, Alder, 41
Young, Reverend W. R., 68
Young Men's Temperance and Literary Society Association, 71, 72

ABOUT THE AUTHOR OF
ANTIOCH TO THE TWENTIES

Elise S. Benyo at her teacher's desk 1971

ELISE SCHOTT BENYO was born in Salt Lake City, Utah, daughter of two native Californians, Franklin T. Schott, son of Adelia B. Kimball and John Schott of Antioch, and Catherine B. Meyer of Sonoma County.

Mrs. Benyo received her A.B. in history and her teaching credential from the University of Utah in 1935. She did graduate work at the University of California at Berkeley. She taught at West and South High Schools in Salt Lake City until February 1946, when she and her husband, Michael Benyo, just discharged from the Army Air Force after World War II, moved to Antioch. She had been vacationing in California ever since she can remember and has many fond memories of the beauty of "traditional" California. She is the mother of three, and the grandmother of three.

History has always been of deep interest to her. She researched the material for the history of Antioch used in the Centennial of July, 1951. She is the past president of the Antioch: Woman's Club during its fiftieth year and updated the Club's history as part of the celebration in February, 1952. She is a founder and past president of the Antioch Branch of the American Association of University Women.

Since 1955 she has been teaching in the Antioch School District.

Mrs. Benyo has great faith in the young people of today. She feels they are thinking and are concerned.

[Editor's note: Narrative biography from the original back cover of the first edition, 1972.]

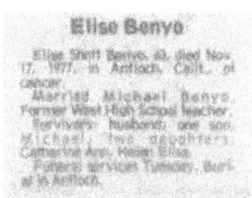

Elise Benyo obituary 1977.

Elise Benyo Grave Marker, Oakview Cemetery, Antioch.

ABOUT THE ANTIOCH HISTORICAL SOCIETY

Antioch Historical Society Logo

MISSION STATEMENT

The Society was founded in 1974 by a group of local citizens. Its purpose is to collect and protect historical artifacts and resources of cultural and historic value or significance relative to the City of Antioch and its sphere of influence. Through operation of a historical museum and through exhibitions of Antioch history the Society shall promote public awareness and appreciation for the heritage of Antioch. It shall also try to provide opportunities for education and scholarship.

THE "HISTORY" IN ANTIOCH HISTORICAL SOCIETY

The Museum is housed since 1999 in the original Riverview Union High School Building. The beautiful brick building houses our various collections. They include a California Delta Room, Military Room, Sports Legends Room, Schools Room and others. We feature a railroad caboose, fire house, and cook house on the grounds. Rooms are available for civic and private parties. Our multipurpose room and theatre provide a wonderful meeting or dining venue for any event. The Society hosts several history days throughout the year featuring and honoring our diverse cultural history. We are 150 years in the making and making history still.

The Antioch Historical Society is identified as a 501(c)3 by the Internal Revenue Service. We welcome your visits, participation in history, membership sponsorship of a room, donations and contributions. Please join us.

THE ANTIOCH HISTORICAL MUSEUM
Hours: Wednesday and Saturday, 1 p.m. to 4 p.m. year-round
Admission: Always free
Address: 1500 West 4th Street, Antioch, Contra Costa County, California, 94509
Telephone: (925) 757–1326
Website: *https://AntiochHistoricalMuseum.org*

QR Code—Antioch Historical Society Website

SACRAMENTO-SAN JOAQUIN

DELTA

NATIONAL HERITAGE AREA

www.ingramcontent.com/pod-product-compliance
Lightning Source LLC
Chambersburg PA
CBHW061140230426
43663CB00027B/2989